"This book, which addresses college advisors and counselors, faculty, and parents, is the key to uniting a team of support for any college student with autism. Dr. Duggan has given us an accessible, upbeat, and realistic guide, with clear advice for a wide range of challenging situations."

—*Karin Evans, Ph.D., Professor of English,*
College of DuPage

"Dr. Michael Duggan has been a dedicated and effective advocate for students on the autism spectrum and their families for over 20 years. He has created the ultimate guide to show how to assist these students and their families with the daunting task of the transition from high school to college. This book is a compassionate, step-by-step companion for college counselors and aspiring college students to deal with everything from friendships, romance, academic success to disability support services."

—*Maria Rago, Ph.D., Clinical Psychologist*

"I had the good fortune to work with Michael at the College of DuPage and saw the beginnings of his work with Autismerica. This amazing book translates his experiences into practical tips for anyone working with students on the spectrum who want to provide a supportive, successful environment. Highly recommend!"

—*Dr. Lisa Stock, Dean of Academic Affairs,*
Ellsworth Community College

First Class Support
for College Students
on the
Autism Spectrum

Michael W. Duggan

First Class Support for College Students on the Autism Spectrum

Practical Advice for College Counselors and Educators

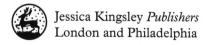
Jessica Kingsley *Publishers*
London and Philadelphia

First published in 2018
by Jessica Kingsley Publishers
73 Collier Street
London N1 9BE, UK
and
400 Market Street, Suite 400
Philadelphia, PA 19106, USA

www.jkp.com

Library of Congress Cataloging in Publication Data
A CIP catalog record for this book is available from the Library of Congress

British Library Cataloguing in Publication Data
A CIP catalogue record for this book is available from the British Library

ISBN 978 1 78592 413 2
eISBN 978 1 78450 777 0

Printed and bound in the United States

Contents

Acknowledgments

There are so many people for me to thank that it's hard to know where to begin. I thank my immediate family—my loving partner Wayne, who has stood by me for all the ups and downs of my life, always being patient and loving and believing in me when I can't even believe in myself. My deceased father Donald, who I now realize gave me many gifts including my sense of humor. My mother Kathleen, for teaching me how beautiful love can be and how important it is to be there for one another, no matter what. Also, my ability to smile and keep a song in my heart most certainly came from her.

I also thank my circle of closest friends who encouraged me and made me laugh when I needed to—Andrew Morris, for being my brother when I needed one; Cathleen Conway, for knowing me better than anyone in the world, including my bad parts; Carol Conway, for being the best second mom ever; Judy Joslin, for being the epitome of class and wisdom while encouraging me at a time early in my career when I needed guidance and confidence the most. When I didn't believe in myself—you did—and I owe you so very much for this. Allen Newkirk, for being the person who is always there to listen and lift me up; Dana Thompson, for being my adored colleague in the Counseling Center, which I call home; Jan Guzi and Libusa Nagyova Guzi, for being such loving friends; Brian Dobbelaere, for being so lovable and sweet; my dog Mocha, for lots of kisses and rarely asking to go potty past bedtime; Richard McCarron, for his amazing meals and even bigger heart; Scott Haldeman, for being the person who can always make me laugh and feel loved no matter how bad things are; Manny and Peggy du Mont, for being the most amazing neighbors a person could ask for; Maren McKellin, for introducing me to Temple Grandin; and obviously, Temple Grandin herself, for being such an inspiration and allowing me to use her photo in my book. I also want to thank Dr. Jocelyn Harney for taking a chance on me many years ago and hiring me for the position I hold and treasure today; Sandra Werner for being the professional mentor when I first began my position and whom was the greatest role model of a counselor and professor one could ever ask for; Amy Teschner, my personal editor, for this book would never have been possible without her amazing work; and Sheryl Ebersold, my Autismerica confidante, who was always there to bounce new ideas off of, challenge me to push myself more than I thought I could, and always be the solid expert in the field when I needed one. You are all like family to me and I love you so.

Finally, I'd like to thank all the students and parents I've had the honor to work with through the years. I've learned a great deal because of you. Every day you ask questions that make me think, grow, and laugh. I feel honored to have been allowed to be a part of your lives and to be there, both when you fail and when you achieve. Your courage and spirit invigorate me every day, and without you my career would mean nothing. Also thank you to all the parents who have worked with me or even against me at times, reminding me at their core they only want the best for their children. Your love and dedication are truly powerful.

May everyone be as blessed as I have been to have the experiences and career I have had up to this point. To everyone who has played a part, I will be forever grateful.

Preface

Before we begin I should tell you a little about myself. To be honest, I didn't begin my adult life planning to be a counselor with a specialty in disabilities. Originally, I was going to be a musician. My background is in jazz music, and I have played various instruments since I was three years old. I began college on a music scholarship, and my primary instrument was the bass trombone, with an emphasis on jazz improvisation—that's the area of music where you go on a stage and listen to a few background chords, and then make up music as you go. I always loved the challenge of creating something out of nothing, and hence I loved improv.

My life changed, as random as this sounds, when I took an anthropology course during my undergraduate studies at Butler University in Indianapolis with Professor Leslie Sharp. We studied a variety of subjects, and among them was the culture of disability. I became fascinated by Deaf culture and communication, the history of Braille and the technological innovations that later translated into the modern world, and the nation-wide advocacy movements spawned by the Americans with Disabilities Act. I could also relate on many other levels to the challenges of being judged when one has an invisible disability that cannot be seen, but once exposed, provokes all kinds of judgments.

As part of an advanced class, I conducted an anthropological study where I staged a fake car accident and lived in a wheelchair for two weeks. I didn't tell anybody, but I wanted to better understand what the disability experience was like—even if on a very low level. As part of my research, each evening I interviewed someone with a disability—learning disabilities, schizophrenia, cerebral palsy, hard of hearing, blindness—and discovered all kinds of information about their lives. I also learned from the way I was treated; people looked down on me, pitied me, and viewed me as "less than" more than I could have imagined. I also found some of my most favorite haunts were less than accessible to someone in a wheelchair. When I concluded my study, I dropped my scholarship, changed my major, and decided to pursue a career working with people with disabilities.

Long story short, I finished my bachelor's degree in psychology and sociology/anthropology, and then my master's degree in rehabilitation (disability) counseling. I was lucky enough to get an assistantship in the college's disability access office, and fell in love with the profession. Again, creativity was an essential skill. I would need to find how to make an art appreciation class accessible to a student with low vision, empower a student who was dyslexic to complete an elementary education internship, or help a student with a communication impairment successfully complete a speech class— all kinds of creative access puzzles. I was absolutely hooked. Upon graduation, I got my first job directing a disability access program at a community college in Oregon. At the time, the college's president had a less than positive view of disability issues, fearing the costs. A colleague warned me that "if you build it, they will come" was the driving philosophy. I took this prediction not as a threat, but as a challenge.

Through a variety of grant writing and collaborations (along with some of the most talented grant writers in the universe), our program grew from a 1.5-employee office serving roughly a hundred students to a 20-employee operation serving more than five hundred. We offered scholarships, tutoring, mentoring, and saw more students graduate than ever. The only downside was that as the program grew, my administrative responsibilities grew as well, and my direct contact with students diminished.

After about seven years, I wanted to be closer to my immediate family. I took a job in the Midwest, and have been there ever since— almost 14 years now. In my current position I am not an administrator, but a counselor. I love this job most of all because every day I work with new students, and they allow me to be a part of the challenges they face. While the students themselves deserve all the credit for their achievements, I am honored to have been part of the process along the way. Every day I start by hoping I can apply what I've learned in the past to help the students I see, and also hope I can learn a few new things that I can use to help those I will see in the future.

I hope that this book will in some small way serve this purpose of ongoing support for students. I am deeply grateful to the incredible colleagues who have encouraged and inspired me along the way, and maybe this book will have a similar effect on its audience. Thanks for reading.

Chapter 1

My First Failure

Asperger's syndrome is a nebulous topic, and therefore difficult to write about. Normally when I first meet a set of parents with a child who has Asperger's, one of their questions is, "How long have you worked with children with autism?" I respond that I have been in the field for more than 20 years, and working specifically with students on the autism spectrum for about 15 of them. Although I've been a therapist for adults with disabilities for a very long time, it really wasn't until I had years of experience under my belt that I could begin putting the pieces together and identify behavioral trends and helpful interventions that were not only practical but also sensitive to the needs of everyone involved. Let me provide an example.

My first year on the job I met with a student named Harry[1] and his father. I was fresh out of graduate school, and although we certainly read about autism, and I passed many an examination on the topic, as almost anyone in a therapeutic the profession will tell you, there is a big difference between studying a diagnosis in a textbook and encountering someone with that diagnosis in real life! At my first meeting with Harry he demonstrated an extremely negative and angry attitude, and, to me at the time, his father seemed equally unenthusiastic and pessimistic. Harry had messed-up hair, an unappealing body odor, and a Transformers shirt on that had seen far better days/belonged in the ragbag. As I asked questions about Harry, what he liked to do, and who he was as a person, I got one-word responses like "okay," "yeah," and "nope." Harry also clearly did not want to be in the office with me that day, and was perfectly okay with his father doing all the talking.

---

1   Please note all names have been changed to protect the anonymity of those mentioned in this book.

Harry's father looked tired. Better dressed than his son, but tired. He would also get upset with Harry whenever Harry didn't give me a complete answer to a question, or gave me one that was off topic. Harry's father explained these behavioral issues often carried over to the classroom, that Harry frequently interrupted his instructors to ask questions that were unrelated to the classwork, or so highly advanced that they demonstrated he had a better grasp of the subject than the instructor. Of course, this audacity was causing problems at school.

Harry's father had asked the school administrators if he could attend the class with Harry, to intervene when Harry was inappropriate and to correct him. I knew from a Section 504/legal[2] (which we will discuss later in Chapter 3) perspective that this is not considered a reasonable request, so I immediately went on the defensive: "How would this be fair to the other students who could not bring their parents? What if there aren't enough desks? How will the instructor react?" I can think of many other poorly worded questions that I targeted in the same direction. I fell into a trap that many people in my field fall into. Rather than looking at the problem itself and brainstorming a solution to it, we invest our energy shooting down the parent's idea. This response turns the relationship into an adversarial one in which the parent feels unheard, the student feels invisible, and the provider becomes exhausted. It's an approach that will almost always lead to failure.

Today I approach these first-time interactions very differently. Harry's father was asking to be in the classroom because he thought it was the only solution to the problem. He felt Harry's disability was unique, particularly in the way it impacted Harry, which he was right to think. He had come to believe that he was the only one who could help Harry break through Harry's behavioral wall. This assumption about his own singular role is where Harry's father was getting it wrong. But you can't blame him, because probably nobody had ever tried to help him break down the wall.

If I were to handle this first meeting with Harry and his father the way I approach such meetings today, I would have started by asking

---

2   See www2.ed.gov/about/offices/list/ocr/504faq.html

Harry's dad for permission to get to know Harry. I often find with students on the spectrum that they have a "hook"—a topic that the person really is an expert in. Most often, these hooks are centered on either video games or Japanese anime, but they can take on other forms too. Past hooks I've found include cars, trains, airplane routings, geography, horror movies; the list goes on and on. These hooks are often a key to communication, a microcosm of expertise that allows the person to feel fully in knowledge, proud, confident, and in control.

And the creation of this anchor in a storm, if you will, makes perfect sense. When we look at adults on the autism spectrum, at the years they spent growing up, there's much that is out of their control. Social relationships are confusing, and can lead to being misunderstood, bullying, alienation, and loneliness. Then with many on the spectrum, you also face the struggles of sensory overload. We know that a large number of adults on the spectrum—which, depending on the research you read, can be anywhere from 25 to 80 percent of them—struggle with a feeling of amplified anxiety to the tenth degree. While I don't suffer from sensory overload, let me try to explain it by using the words my students have given to me.

Let's say you walk into a typical classroom where an instructor is giving a lecture. In that room there might be a mild hum coming from an overhead projector, probably the whispers of students sitting in the back of the classroom, random noises from the occasional dropped pen or turning of a page, clicks on laptop keyboards, and the footsteps of people passing in the hallway outside the door, or maybe farther away still, construction noise. While all these things are going on, most of us are cognitively able to ignore these typical sounds and focus on the lecture at hand. But a person with sensory overload hears all this noise at an equal level of volume. The noises outside the classroom are every bit as loud as the professor's words. You can imagine how tiring this would be! Now take this sensation of clamor, and apply it to every place the person goes—from the hallway, to the cafeteria, to the car, to home.

Now, not every person has sensory overload to this extreme. Autism is a spectrum disorder. I always emphasize this word "spectrum" because autism does vary a lot from person to person. Regardless of the degree of overload being mild or severe, it is nonetheless *always* taxing. Just as a headache can register from a 1 to a 10 in severity, any headache that never goes away will impact a person's day-to-day functioning.

Back to hooks. When a person suffers from overload (to any degree), it makes sense to seek a place where it is possible to tune out all the noise, the distractions, and the confusion—a retreat where there is no unpredictability, a universe that is ever growing, but safe because it is theirs to discover and theirs to explain. Most often I find my students will explore their world of hooks in their rooms—a place that is probably quiet, where there are no noises or distractions to take them away from their focus. It makes perfect sense.

So, of course, I would immediately want to identify and understand Harry's hook, and figure out the ways he can take the feeling of comfort he draws from studying that hook to places and situations outside of his room, and into the classroom. The goal is not to create a way for him to leave the world of the classroom and retreat to a different place, but to begin to show him there are ways to feel safe away from home, and more importantly, to show him there are individuals in the world other than his immediate family he can trust to go into it with him.

You see, parents are natural experts on hooks. How could they not be? A student's hook is most often that child's favorite topic of conversation, and parents want to have a connection to their child. To parents, learning about hooks is innate—we do everything we can as parents to be a part of our child's world because we love them so much. But this pursuit often pushes against the belief among socially cultured adults that most people in the outside world don't want to hear about Pokémon or Transformers, so parents might shield others from these topics in an effort to be polite. The result, though, can be young people with autism deciding that their only trustworthy connection to the outside world is their parents, and maybe, if they're lucky, other young adults on the spectrum with interest in the same or closely related hooks.

The hook is therefore incredibly important for me as a therapist. It's my entryway into establishing a connection with Harry, and hopefully with his parents as well. I'm willing to take an hour or two out of what might seem like utterly unproductive time given the pressing issues at hand to teach both Harry and his parents that others are capable of understanding him, and if we can develop this degree of trust with one another, perhaps Harry and I can then begin to transition into discussions about inappropriate behaviors, and develop cues to recognize how his actions and words might be off-putting and interfering with instruction in the classroom.

As human beings, we are taught at an early age that there is good and bad, right and wrong, heroic and evil. And these simple dualities are shoved down our throats as soon as we can begin to understand the most basic of words. The majority of cartoons, fairy tales, and television shows all teach the same fundamental lessons. Not that this teaching is entirely bad; there are many valuable moral lessons to be gleaned from these stories. But they also tell us that when we observe behavior that we don't like, or that veers off the course of basic lessons in so-called correct behavior, it must be coming from a bad place.

If we're honest with ourselves, how many of us see a crying child on an airplane or in a restaurant and blame the parent? "If they were stricter, or less strict, or had better parenting skills, their child would shut up," we think. Even if only unconsciously. This belief system falls into almost everything, even to us as therapists and educators. So, when we meet with Harry and his father, we hear Harry's inappropriate comments, and the unreasonable requests of Harry's father, and we label them as wrong, even bad. We shift into a negative mindset, and it's downhill from there. We often fail to think that perhaps Harry is acting out because it's the only way he thinks he *can* interact with the outside world, and that Harry's father is not asking for special dispensations to be difficult, but because he truly believes they offer the only possible way for Harry to have any hope of living an independent life, when Harry's father is gone.

I hope that at this point we've identified where some of the breakdowns occurred in that first meeting, but remember, I work as a therapist with students at college level. What if people attending every IEP (Individualized Education Program) meeting, or all the teachers, or all the administrators, don't put these pieces together? If they don't, it certainly doesn't mean any one of them is a bad person.

Special education instructors and the administrators who supervise their programs are some of the greatest unsung heroes in the world. While I had the luxury of spending an hour, even several hours, with just Harry and his father, most special education professionals are afforded the opportunity to spend only 15 minutes with them both because they have 20 or more students with other behavioral issues to deal with, 30 sets of IEP paperwork forms to fill out, 15 phone calls to return, and endless emails. The American special education system is a broken one where the expectations for success have become so unrealistic that even Wonder Woman (or Superman?) could not meet every need for every child. People fall through the cracks—how could they not?

So here you are, reading this book. Most likely you're a professional of some sort—you might be a therapist, a college professor, or maybe even a university dean, and you begin to get nervous—"So what hope is there?" and, "If you're saying these kids will fall through the cracks, what do we do?" I wish I had all the answers, but I don't. In this book, I am going to share the backgrounds of students like Harry, and the lessons I've learned, all in the hope that you recognize glimmers of someone you care for, or someone you work with. Frankly, Harry did fall through the cracks in working with me, because I didn't know the right questions to ask and neither did his parents. But I've gotten better at my job. Through insight, kindness, and experience, I have seen countless Harrys graduate from college, or trade school, or even get a job at a local company without going to college, and they are leading happy lives. We know more about autism, and the autism spectrum, now than we did just 15 years ago, and 15 years from now we'll know even more. The world is full of Harrys, and if we ask the right questions, we can open numerous doors for them.

Chapter 2

The Phantom Success Story

Often students on the spectrum fall through the cracks when they get into college. The dangerous and prevailing assumption is that the expectations and rigor from high school will remain much the same in college. I find this idea especially prevalent in the case of community colleges, where the belief is that somehow, because it is a community college, standards and expectations might be lower for students, a perception that couldn't be further from the truth. This is actually a trap most Americans fall into, as I did my first year at university. For students on the spectrum, however, the transition to college can be especially arduous, and if it isn't planned properly, it will nearly always lead to first semester failure.

Take Aiden, a very charming young man who was also on the handsome side. I think conventional good looks can work against some adults on the spectrum, as people around them tend to overlook the significance of their symptoms, at least early on. Aiden had a pleasant personality, would smile when appropriate, and did a good job maintaining eye contact, although upon closer examination you could see it tended to follow a formulaic pattern that often higher-functioning Asperger's adults rely on.

Aiden wanted to go into the computer industry and had many of the loves that adults on the spectrum have: video games, science fiction, anime, etc. In terms of high school performance Aiden also seemed well equipped for success. He had a C to B grade point average, decent ACT scores, and all kinds of positive comments written in his IEP documentation. It seemed like he would have little-to-no problem succeeding in college and would require little help.

But once Aiden started college classes, things began to break down. While he was able to live at home with his family, which proved convenient, homework assignments were often late and completed improperly, with a rushed tone. Examination grades were low. Attendance was good overall, although he was often late to class. It's interesting to note none of these details were discovered till near the end of his first semester, because when anyone asked him how his courses were going, he would report back "Great!" and truly in his mind, he thought he was in good academic shape. He certainly wasn't lying or being distrustful about his work, because he was working from a different definition of academic success than the one that dominated his new college environment.

In the American secondary special education system, the prevailing determinate of success is attendance. Because high school students with disabilities are often clustered in resource classrooms, where levels of functioning can be wide-ranging, it's hard to determine standards. However, students who are mainstreamed in traditional classrooms often receive breaks from instructors because of their charming quirkiness and high-functioning intellects. They are able to remember enough to get C grades on exams, tend to have sterling attendance, and really do make an effort in class to be fully present, which any teacher is grateful for. And there's often extra credit for an extra push if needed. All of these factors rolled together enable a really likable person on the spectrum to make it through.

College is different. Most classes don't factor attendance into the grade at all. Examinations tend to make up a large portion of the grade, extra credit might not be an option, and even homework may have a minimal impact. For example, at the college where I teach, math instructors often assign math homework but do not grade it and do not include it when calculating a student's final grade. The students are still expected to complete it, and are given answer keys to grade themselves, but it is optional with regard to course grades. Students who do the homework tend to be very successful. It's thoughtfully designed and does a nice job in re-iterating the day's lecture, but it is optional nonetheless. Other disciplines in college may take a similar approach to homework.

Such changes to the rules set up Aiden to fail. First, the most important element for previous success, attendance, is no longer a variable. And while the nonspectrum student may be able to make the necessary determinations and adjustments a few weeks in, for a student who often bases behaviors on *rules* rather than *patterns*, it's extremely confusing, especially over many weeks and months. In some college classes, homework assignments might be part of the grade, but to a lower degree than in high school. Aiden would do his homework, but often not to a point of thorough completion. Again, having to finish the homework for whatever credit it might provide is a break in the rules Aiden has been taught. In a high school resource room, just turning something in can often be viewed as a victory. Or if Aiden was in an integrated setting, he might have gotten a poor grade on his homework, but with a little extra credit he would probably still squeak by.

Another challenging change in the rules for Aiden came with homework that was recommended but not required. *Recommended* is a gray word to Aiden. He tends to look at things as black and white and driven by rules. So, Aiden wasn't doing his homework in those classes where it wasn't required, and saw nothing wrong with that perfectly rational behavior.

So now we have Aiden, who has gone to every class and turned in the required homework, facing a final letter grade based perhaps 80 to 100 percent on examinations. Aiden wasn't the best test taker in high school either, but his memory skills, plus all the differences mentioned previously, would compensate for his faults. But now relying on a range of factors is no longer viable. Aiden gets Ds and Fs on his exams, and at the end of the semester, he ends up with a low D grade point average.

When the D arrives, Aiden is mystified. His parents are also confused, saying, "You said you were doing well in your classes!" And to Aiden, things *were* going well. He was attending class, he did the required assignments, and if extra credit had been offered (which it wasn't), he would have done it. Aiden is just as frustrated as his parents. The question now on everyone's mind is, "What happened?"

When I meet with Aiden and his family, we start with a reality check. Together we acknowledge the change in rules since high school, and we put new mechanisms in place. Academic accommodations available through higher education will not be enough to solve the problem—although he probably didn't have access to any of these accommodations anyway.[1] It's important to realize that in higher education there are those "have to" things that legally must be provided to a student with a disability in college, and then those "need to" things that are not legally required, but still need to be secured. We will talk more about these additional resources later.

So, at this juncture, we need to take a more proactive stance on Aiden's behalf. We have to seek out instructors who have a policy of open office hours. I cannot emphasize this necessity enough. Sometimes when I say this, a faculty member thinks I'm saying we're looking for "easy" instructors—not at all. In fact, sometimes instructors who are open for lots of discussion are a college's toughest graders. But we have to remember, intellectual capabilities are not the issue for these students; it's the lack of social skills and structural design that causes their failure. Faculty who are open to regular dialogue to clarify information become essential to their success—especially early on in a college career.

If you, as a professional, can't find someone at college who can help you in identifying these faculty, the website Rate My Professors (www.ratemyprofessors.com) can be genuinely helpful. Students themselves rate instructors and include comments regarding their experiences with individual teachers. The site is not monitored (other than for racist/sexist/homophobic/abusive messages), and does not allow the faculty member to respond. It is controversial for many people in higher education, and rightfully so. It is an unfair, biased site,

---

1   For answers to frequently asked questions about the rights of students with disabilities, see the US Department of Education website (Office for Civil Rights) at www2.ed.gov/ about/offices/list/ocr/504faq.html

and we, as human beings, can be infamous for lying or crossing the line when we think we have been slighted.

For your purposes, however, you aren't visiting Rate My Professors to look for comments like "easy" or "no work required." You're looking for instructors who make themselves available— dedicated professionals who do everything they can to help their students succeed. You want to find instructors who have passion and excitement for what they do. Don't be scared if people say an instructor at your college is "hard." Have faith in the students you work with; it's not the level of difficulty, but the organization that matters. Also, if you find an instructor with multiple positive comments, and then read a bad review or two, don't let that scare you. Nobody gets a 100 percent positive rating.

So we find faculty who are open for meeting with Aiden regularly, and we present this plan for better communication with professors to Aiden, and then we have one of the most important, and forgotten, conversations in any young student's future: Does Aiden want to be here? You see, this is a question that too often goes unasked. In the secondary system, and for the most part in American culture, completing high school is a given. We have an unspoken understanding that to accomplish anything in life one needs to have at least a diploma, and given the current economic forecast that's mostly true, but college is different.

I remember another student I worked with, named Erin. Erin had one of the highest ACT scores I had ever seen. She had straight As in high school, and although she struggled with basic social interaction, was clearly a very bright young woman. She worked as a register operator at the local grocery store for many years, and was so efficient and helpful in her job that she was one of the store's most valuable employees, earning her a full-time position as a register operator when she finished high school. She turned the position down to go to college.

Erin easily finished her studies and earned her associate's degree. She then transferred to another university and completed a bachelor's degree and was fully prepared to enter her profession. In her first job, however, she hated the work she did. She worked in the business world where there was a much larger requirement of social interaction and unpredictability, and the closest job she could find was more than 30 miles from her home, requiring that she rely on public transportation. Her commute was over two hours long. The job didn't work out. She then found another job closer to home, but with a similar result.

Erin and her mother came to meet with me, feeling very lost. Her mother said Erin was very depressed, and rarely off of her computer. She also had little interest in looking for a new job, and seemed to want to remain living at home permanently. We talked about when Erin was happiest, and when she felt the most fulfilled. She said she missed the days when she worked for many years at her old grocery store. As a temporary fix, we were able to get her old job back. Her personality returned, her performance was exceptional, within a few months she again was offered a full-time position, and accepted it. While she was not earning as much money as she had in her degree-level position, it was enough to live on, in combination with qualifying for independent living assistance through the state, and she had health benefits. Most importantly, she was happy. In time her mother grew to accept the situation. I learned an important lesson from Erin's experience: we must not superimpose our values onto others. The definition of a full life is different for each person.

So, back to Aiden. We had the discussion regarding whether he really wanted to be in college. And if the answer was yes, was he prepared to take the steps necessary and put the effort in to be successful? Indeed, he said he wanted to be successful, but didn't know how. Everyone in the room was greatly relieved to hear the desire was there, and he just needed our help.

Now that we had established that Aiden wanted to do well in college, and we had found faculty who had open office hours and were keen to answer questions, we put a plan in place. First, it was important that Aiden understand the expectations accompanying each and every class he took, all the requirements *for him to be successful*. This would be the key phrase for determining the work he needed to do. We agreed at the end of each class, for just a couple minutes after everyone had left, that he would ask and answer the question, resulting in the statement, "For me to be successful, I need to..." and he would fill in the information based on what he had heard during class.

Once this list was established, we agreed upon a regular homework routine, a daily time he would do it, and a place where he could work with as minimal distractions as possible. (I would not recommend public places with excessive noise, bedrooms, or classrooms just before or after class. These are all places that are riddled with distractions and can hinder the ability to focus.)

Depending upon the student's manageable level of accountability (and parents need to be honest with themselves about this), ideally the place would be another room in the house where there is as little distraction as possible. There should be no TVs, no cell phones, and if a laptop is required, parent and child should reach an agreement that they will only access those websites connected to the coursework at hand. Saving the browsing history can be helpful for this. While I realize this sounds like the establishment of a police state, it's necessary for establishing a pattern of behavior. Once a solid homework routine is set, the student can be successful all the way to a PhD.

So, we established that from 4 to 6 pm each day, Aiden would do his work in the dining room. If more time was required, the added minutes or hours could be negotiated for the lifting of other household chores later. Aiden agreed that before 4 pm each day he would show his mom the list of work required for him to be successful. While Aiden's mother was concerned about the time required from her to review the list each day, and the level of dependency it would create, I assured her it would be only a few weeks until the reporting would not be necessary.

In addition to addressing the homework, we agreed we all needed to be on the right page about understanding how Aiden's grade would be calculated. We made copies of the pages from each syllabus that detailed each course's final grade, and put these copies everywhere— magnetized to the fridge, in Aiden's bedroom, and programmed into his phone. I had a copy as well. Each time a grade was entered in, we all added this information to our copies. We would then add those numbers together so Aiden always knew where his grade was landing. This vigilance helped Aiden in establishing a feeling of control over his situation, and helped his parents feel less in the dark about his performance.

With all these strategies in place, we began the semester. The change wasn't immediate. At first, Aiden struggled with keeping the structure of his schedule, sneaking his phone into his study sessions, and occasionally not following up with his instructors after class because he wanted to be one of the first in line for the cafeteria. But in time, a pattern was established. Aiden began to develop structure. He began to understand what a good grade was, and his grades started to slowly turn upward.

I emphasized with Aiden's parents the importance of positive reinforcement. I'm a big believer in rewarding good behavior in a distinct and memorable way. Aiden's family agreed that every Thursday night, if Aiden was successful that week, he could dictate what they had for dinner. It was a small reward, but again, part of a pattern that could become predictable. I forget what meal it was they agreed upon, but hopefully it wasn't something too unhealthy like fried chicken or macaroni and cheese, to avoid other health issues!

Once we had this behavioral pattern established, it was amazing how quickly it fell into place without much intervention. Each semester we would work to establish the pattern, as each instructor might have a different communication style, but in time, Aiden was able to translate this process into almost any course. There was still the occasional bump along the way (group projects, field trips, take-home exams), but we were now taking the seemingly multicomplex world of higher education and making it more quantifiable and organized.

Chapter 3

The First Year of College

What to Expect and How to Help Students Succeed

At this point, theoretically at least, everything should be in place for the transition out of high school. With a little advocacy and planning, that chapter of young adults' lives can wrap up nicely. But what should families expect from the college or university itself? And when specifically should they apply, secure financial aid, take placement tests, and complete the other tasks necessary to enroll in college? What can be expected from the college or university once life there really gets underway? And what steps need to be taken to ensure that life there goes well? I hope this chapter will help you and your student plan those steps. The first thing I want to do is outline a timeline of what you should do, when. Then we will go into detail about what to expect and accomplish in each step.

Here is a timeline I recommend for students before arrival to higher education:

Junior year of high school
Have the realistic talk about whether college is the next logical step.

Summer after end of junior year of high school
Visit different colleges and universities you are considering. Schedule visits ahead of time and meet with each school's disability

services office, counseling center, and admissions office for a campus tour. Schedule this visit at least a month in advance to ensure all your appointments can happen on the same day, and that the day goes smoothly.

Senior year of high school

Choose a college to transfer to and begin college applications. Focus IEP/Section 504 transition planning on making this transition a reality. Also take ACT/SAT tests in the early fall to ensure plenty of time to receive scores for applications. Note: If you require accommodations for these exams, arranging them can take more time, so start planning even earlier. Investigate any state vocational rehabilitation services available in your area. Vocational rehabilitation is a state-wide agency in every territory of the US that provides funds for adults with disabilities to find training and/or employment. For more information about the specific services offered in your state, visit rsa.ed.gov.

October of senior year of high school

If you plan to apply for financial aid, fill out and submit the Free Application for Federal Student Aid (FAFSA). The form is available on fafsa.gov on October 1.

January of senior year of high school

Apply for admission into whatever university or community college you would like to attend.

February of senior year of high school

Begin to receive acceptances into colleges and universities. Make an appointment with the designated advisor for the school you intend to visit.

March of senior year of high school

Take whatever additional placement exams are necessary for registering for college classes. Meet with college advisor to discuss course requirements. Submit whatever additional forms might be necessary for financial aid processing. Schedule an appointment with your college's disability services office to arrange academic accommodations after registering for classes in April.

April of senior year of high school

Receive financial aid award letter if applicable. Meet with college advisor or other representative a second time to register for classes. Meet with the college's disability services office a second time to solidify accommodations, and to get feedback on instructor choices, if possible.

May to first day of college

Enjoy summer. Attend new student orientation. Visit campus and practice getting to campus if using public transportation. Order textbooks for classes. Relax.

In terms of registration dates and deadlines, each school might have slight differences in their schedules, but I find most of these deadlines pretty close to universal. If there is a need for financial aid, I cannot emphasize how important it is to do this application as early in the year as possible. Many states have set pools of grant funds available, and when all the funds are gone, that's it. Ideally parents should have their application done before March 1 of the year they plan for their child to attend, and remember that students can apply to an unlimited amount of schools for financial aid at once if they're waiting for acceptances.

Another question I sometimes get is regarding states' social services. Many states have specialized vocational rehabilitation grant programs for students where the state will pay for part, or all, of the college tuition for a student with a disability. To see what a state offers, Google "vocational rehabilitation" and the state name, and there should be a link to the appropriate website. The benefits of vocational rehabilitation can include assistance with tutoring, help in paying for additional disability-related expenses such as transportation and textbooks, and job placement assistance when the student graduates. While I sometimes hear the wait times for appointments and paperwork can be a little frustrating, the potential benefits far outweigh these minor frustrations.

So let's talk a little more about the two most important appointments (other than talking with the financial aid office, if necessary): academic advising and accommodations planning.

In terms of meeting with an academic advisor, most schools nowadays will allow students to choose from a host of available people either in the student's specific major or from their college's counseling center. Encourage families to do as much research as possible to find a good fit. It's okay to email advisors ahead of time and ask them questions. Make sure they have some background in advising students on the spectrum, or students with disabilities in general, and parents should ask what help they can expect to receive from that person. The timeliness of their response and answers to questions can be good clues as to whether that advisor will be a good fit. Parent networking can also be *very* helpful in this area, such as going to events where other parents are in attendance to pick their brains for advisors they recommend.

In a first meeting with an advisor, the requirements for graduation should be clearly spelt out, and whatever placement test requirements exist as well. Some schools will waive placement test exams with qualifying ACT/SAT scores, so see if this is also a policy as well. The goal is for a family to walk out of that meeting with at least a basic idea of the classes needed to take for the fall. Between the first and second meeting with an advisor, families should begin to drill down into more detail by looking at specific days and times as well as instructors (remember Rate My Professors and related websites, as discussed in Chapter 2), and most importantly, have open parent–child discussions about what classes interest the student.

If a student has a specific major in mind, there might be a nonnegotiable predetermined plan of courses. In this case, there isn't a lot of latitude. If the student is undecided, though, help look for a combination of courses they must have to graduate (math, English, science, etc.), and some classes in areas they find personally interesting, even if they might not be transferable to other majors.

For example, if I have a student who *loves* video games (and I have many), we might register for a couple of "gen ed" classes in math and English, but add a video game design course, even if the class is well outside their major. I find the most important term of college hands down is the very first—it usually sets the tone for the entirety of their studies, so a combination of practical courses and interesting ones is ideal.

In terms of the number of classes a first year student on the spectrum should take, the decision depends on a variety of factors. I always recommend starting on the lighter side if possible, although sometimes the cost of college or scholarship programs requires a student attend full-time or more than full-time, whether that's desirable or not. If there is some flexibility, I find two to three required courses like English and math and one or two fun classes like a physical education class, music, art, or a computer class can provide a nice balance. We are trying more than anything else to build positive momentum.

Sometimes it happens that a student misses the deadlines and registers very late in the summer, and sometimes life just happens and it's impossible to register sooner. This delay can put the student in a tough place where first-, or even second-choice classes are full, and the only options are classes that take place on a Saturday or a course-load of evening classes. Should this happen, I recommend the student takes a term off entirely, or if they must attend, going with a light load. I've had students rush into terrible course schedules with only night classes because those are the only classes available, then fail everything, and not earn any credits. Even worse, the bad schedule leads to fear and a negative attitude toward college that can take years to undo. Encourage planning ahead. Encourage students to get the right days, times, and instructors, or they shouldn't go at all until they can. College is just too important (and expensive) to rush into it and fail.

One final point: be realistic about how early or late in the day students can take classes. I will ask a student how early they can start classes. A frequent response might be "12 pm." The parent, then hearing this, frowns and says, "8 am." The truth is, they are probably both off. Going to class too early can lead to oversleeping and anxieties over coming in late. Going too late can lead to losing track of time and missing out as well. For most students on the spectrum, a 9 or 10 am start time is a good beginning, and a cut-off time of around 4 pm works well, especially if they take medication that might lead to fatigue, or there's just a pattern of getting sleepy later in the day.

After the student has chosen classes and registered, they should meet as soon as possible with the college's office of disability services or office of accommodations about what services can be put into place to help. There are certain standard accommodations that most students on the autism spectrum can expect to be eligible for right off the bat, usually including extra time for testing, a quiet area for testing, volunteer and/or paid note-takers who will take notes for a student in class, the ability to record lectures, and priority seating. To be eligible for any services, families need to provide documentation of the disability to the appropriate office, so they should work with medical professionals or previous schools ahead of time to acquire and complete the paperwork needed.

When meeting with the accommodations professional, the student should do as much of the talking as possible. On a basic level, the student needs to learn to advocate for him or herself. Self-advocacy is something they will need their entire life: in their classes, their future job, with their friends and relationships, and even, one day, when their parents are gone. It's never too early to work on communicating one's needs. The second reason is the relationship between these two people is very important. When we look at research on students with disabilities in college, we know nearly half of all students who initially seek out services never ask for help again if left to their own devices.[1]

---

1   Barnett, L. (1996) *Directory of Disability Support Services in Community Colleges.* Washington, DC: American Association of Community Colleges.

Thus, it's very important that young adults develop a comfort level with the advisor, because if that comfort isn't there, then we, as professionals, can forget them ever going to that key person for help. It will *never* happen. When I meet with a parent and student, and the parent does all the talking and answers all the questions, I can almost always guarantee I'll never see the child again unless the parent comes along. That child will not seek me out for him or herself.

A good professional will drift into areas of personal interest, too. I've had students go on ten-minute tangents during our appointments, delving into Pokémon, Halo, and automobiles. Sometimes parents will feel the need to stop a child from speaking, knowing that he or she is talking too much and missing out on the topic at hand. While the parent might be right about that, I say, let it happen anyway. The professional will know when to redirect the conversation, and more importantly, a relationship will develop, so when the unexpected catastrophe does occur, the student feels comfortable enough to reach out and talk about what's really going on.

Remember also that there are services that "have to" happen and those that "need to" happen. "Have to" services are the ones that are required by law (specifically Section 504 of the 1973 Rehabilitation Act in most cases), things like extra time, note-taking, seating, etc. Then there are the services that need to happen, but the college is not required to provide, things like tutoring, mentoring, advocacy assistance, and academic monitoring and support. When a family comes into a meeting expecting both "have to" and "need to" services at the same time, everything gets off on the wrong foot—an adversarial relationship takes hold between the parents and the provider, with the student wanting no part of any of it.

The conversation should start with talking about accommodations and how they are implemented. For example, most students can test in a quiet area with extra time, but need to schedule this accommodation ahead of time. Most students can arrange note-taking assistance in their classes, but the office might have a specific procedure for how to arrange it. After discussions regarding accommodations have occurred, and procedures clarified, both the student and service provider should look at the specific schedule in detail. Does the provider know any of the faculty? Are they accommodating, or not? Remember that this person works with all the faculty of the college, so you probably won't get negative criticism, even if it's warranted. But a good provider might gently suggest, "Mr. Gaston is very knowledgeable of his academic discipline, but perhaps Ms. Conway might be a better fit." If they're lucky, the school they are attending might have a large Deaf community, and there will be sign language interpreters attending classes with students. These interpreters can be great resources. Often, they will share feedback, observed first hand, regarding how instructors work with students. I remember my first day on the job at a new school housed next to the School for the Deaf. I gave the interpreters two highlighters—green and blue. I gave them a complete list of college faculty and asked them to highlight the best faculty in blue, and the not-so-best in green. My sheet was filled with color!

After a schedule is established, and it has been verified that the faculty choices are generally sound ones, you can talk about other possible areas the student may encounter difficulty with. It may not be the role of the disability office to supply this help, but there might be other places on campus that do. If no one on campus can help with these ancillary (but vital) services, the onus is on the family to put them in place. Some specific services families will want to develop a plan for include:

★ Where do I go for help with tutoring in different subjects?

★ If I suspect completing homework is an issue, whom can my child meet with regularly to ensure homework is being completed in a timely manner?

★ Are there any mentoring programs on campus? If not, would you be open to pairing my child up with someone?

★ Where can my child go for help with organizational skills?

As discussed in earlier chapters, the biggest struggle for most students is homework. You want layers of accountability, so find someone the student can report to regularly about progress—ideally not a parent, but better a parent than no one. A pattern of accountability needs to be established and verifiable. If the college the student attends does not offer this kind of service, it is worth it in the long run for the family to consider hiring a paid tutor from the outside who is paid once a week to help establish and track accountability. Within a term or two, there won't be a need for this service, as the student will create a positive pattern.

If the person in charge of tracking accountability does end up being you, the professional, remember to ask to see tangible evidence of progress. Teenagers can lie, or just misperceive the situation, and think they are doing better than they really are. If I had a dime for each time I asked a student if they're doing well and they said "sure," followed by me looking at their grades and seeing otherwise, I'd be a rich man! Update that syllabus with grade calculations every week so there are no surprises at the end of the semester.

If the student plays their cards right, they should be able to enjoy their summer with a registered schedule, arranged financial aid, and solidified accommodations and services. Have no doubt, though, no matter how much planning is done, there will always be the unexpected bump. For now, though, encourage students to relax and enjoy a sense of accomplishment. They (and you) have earned it!

Chapter 4

Anxiety

The Silent Partner

One of the pitfalls of being a professional who works with adults on the autism spectrum is underestimating the role of anxiety as a dual diagnosis. When we step back and think about it, however, the anxiety makes a lot of sense—there's sensory overload and the challenges of social interaction, plus all the increasingly stressful aspects of being a teenager in today's world. Anxiety becomes an inevitable sidebar, but even the most diligent therapist often misses it, because the focus can be so much on the tasks at hand.

I can think of one student I worked with named Sebastian. Sebastian came from a high school that did a pretty decent job in preparing him for college, at least in terms of academics. When we met initially with his parents, most of the questions I asked him led to one-word answers—mostly "yes," "no," or "sometimes"—but that wasn't unusual for a first meeting. Underneath his somewhat typical responses, however, there was a great deal of stress. Sebastian in particular tended to be rule-driven and oriented toward knowing and then meeting expectations, and he felt a strong connection to his high school, so the thought of a new school with all kinds of different expectations and standards was very frightening to him.

One of the differences between high school and college is a varied schedule. A typical day in high school begins and ends at a set time each day. For example, maybe classes begin with homeroom at 8:30 am, and the last class period might be at 2:30 pm with a dismissal at 3:30 pm each day. In college, however, the scheduling becomes very different. Most classes take place either on Monday, Wednesday, and Friday, or on Tuesday and Thursday, with classes running for either 50 minutes three times a week or 75 minutes twice a week, accordingly. Because most colleges equate full-time status with only 12 hours of attendance per week, most students who start their classes early in the morning are done by noon or 1 pm. While most college students enjoy this difference in structure and additional freedom in their schedules, for a student on the spectrum this change can be a stressful shift in pattern.

Additional stressors include all the traditional changes that come from attending a new school: new places to eat; new instructors; few, if any, familiar faces; and if the student is living on campus, an entire host of additional sources of anxiety, including a roommate, following through on daily hygiene rituals, and managing money. Simply put, there's a lot of heavy emotional lifting involved in making the transition to college life.

Speaking of dormitory living, if you are working with a student who lives in a dorm, it is important for you to address eating behaviors. Jennifer attended a university far away from home, and she really struggled with the presentation of food at the cafeteria. It was usually all plopped onto a single plate, and for her, food touching other food was especially stressful—a fairly common struggle among students I've worked with. Jennifer's diet was harmed significantly, as she would eat only those foods that clearly didn't touch other foods, such as cereal, pizza, and solid proteins like chicken breasts. Some days she would go with minimal nutrition, and she lost a lot of weight. This struggle over food put her at a significant disadvantage and affected almost all areas of her life.

Hygiene is another important topic for discussion. Honestly, for most male college students in their college-age years, regardless of disability, hygiene should be addressed ahead of dorm life, but it's particularly critical for students on the spectrum. Students should develop a pattern of all the things they will do in terms of taking care of themselves, including where their self-care will take place. Where will they put on their deodorant? Brush their teeth? Where will they get the water to rinse their mouths? How will they know the deodorant is nearly empty? What will they use for soap, and where will they put it when they are finished bathing? These are all questions to ask and answer before that first day and night away from home.

So, back to Sebastian. Fortunately, I work at a community college, so I didn't need to worry about any dormitory issues for Sebastian, but there were plenty of other stresses associated with his transition. Sebastian was good at articulating his needs, which I applauded. If he felt stressed out, he would be the first to pick up the phone and seek assistance. The problem with him, however, was his reliance on coming to my office four or five times a day, plus calling my voicemail nearly endlessly in between. When I was not available to answer the phone, he was able to get to know our office staff especially well, and would turn to them for support as well. Everyone in our building knew Sebastian, and, while he was a very sweet and lovable guy, it wasn't long until he really began taxing our resources.

He would call with all kinds of concerns, ones that were legitimate, especially to him. Among his questions and concerns: "How do I do a group project when some of my partners aren't pulling their share?" "My teachers have pop quizzes, and that really stresses me out." "I have a paper due on Monday, but I don't allow myself to do more than two hours of work on Sundays, as I think this is an important day for me to rest." "My class next week is meeting in a computer lab in another building, and I'm worried I'll get lost finding it." And so on.

Beyond these constantly new and unexpected transitions were the larger psychological issues I think most community college students go through when they transition from high school: missing their peers from high school, the disconnectedness that comes with not knowing the school staff, anxiety over balancing work, school, and life (if they work), and then the larger existential question regarding what to do with their lives after finishing college. Truly, the cliché that college delivers the best years of our lives does not apply to everyone; college is much more complex than we realize.

For Sebastian, it was all too much. I knew right away we needed to focus on developing strategies for managing the unexpected. We could no longer operate on a one-rule-for-every-day situation but instead needed to come up with what I called Plan A, Plan B, and Plan C. I thought we should focus on just three plans at first so things would not become too overwhelming, and while three plans were not enough to catch everything, they did help reduce Sebastian's phone calls and panic attacks.

Plan A was for when things happened as expected—no major assignments due, no changes in location, no outside work to be expected. Plan B was for when major assignments were due and required the allotment of additional work time, and Plan C was for something completely unexpected. We agreed Sebastian would fill out worksheets each Friday, and only if he had filled them out and emailed them to me that day could we meet to discuss how he was doing. Here are some examples of those worksheets.

Plan A

Homework due this week: Read Chapter 1, answer questions on page 21 and type up answers

When I will do homework: Every Monday–Thursday, 4–6 pm

Locations of classes this week: Always in RHE 1234

Work involving other people: None

Bring to class: Book, homework, folder, notebook, pen

If I'm unsure about something: Email Professor Jones at jones@rrr.edu

Plan B (when larger assignments are due)

Homework due: Take home Midterm on European History, all questions

When I will do homework: BIG part of grade. Monday–Thursday, 4–6 pm AND will need to work Sunday, 1–7 pm

How I will reward myself when done: Slurpee and large sausage pizza Sunday night when finished. Mom will let me use credit card

Locations of classes this week: Always in RHE 1234

Bring to class: Book, homework, folder, notebook, pen, and Midterm

If I'm unsure about something: Email Professor Jones at jones@rrr.edu

If important and still no answer within 4 hours: Email Dr. Duggan at duggan@rrr.edu

Plan C (when the unexpected is happening)

Homework due: Read Chapter 5; type up answers to questions on page 42

When I will do homework: Normal times, Monday–Thursday, 4–6 pm

Unexpected thing happening: Group project; class meeting in Computer Lab Monday in QQQ 1233

What I need to do differently: Make sure over the weekend I know where QQQ 1233 is. Meet with my group Sunday afternoon

Locations of classes this week: QQQ 1233 Monday, rest of week in TTR 4723

If I'm unsure about something: Email Professor Jones at jones@rrr.edu; email group online through portal

If important and still no answer within 4 hours: Email Dr. Duggan at duggan@rrr.edu

This worksheet system didn't work perfectly, but it did help Sebastian gain a sense of control over his situation. Incidentally, you can access these worksheets, along with many others, on my website, at www.michaelwduggan.com. They are free of charge, and you can alter them however you like to meet your needs.

After Sebastian, his parents, and I worked to help him develop structure over his behavior on a daily basis, we could talk about some of the larger pressing issues affecting his quality of life, including making friendships, planning his future, and balancing work and pleasure. These are also important goals, but they take a backseat to preparing for the daily stressors. Remember that the person on the spectrum knows their unique stressors best, and understands the topics it would be best to address ahead of time to alleviate issues that might interfere with success. Below is a list of information students might want to have ahead to assist them as they enroll in college:

★ Where to park

★ Where to get tutoring

★ How/where to access disability services

★ Where to access counseling

★ How to make an appointment to see your counselor

★ How to look up your instructor's office hours

★ Where and when to use the college's health services

★ Where to eat and how to pay

★ How to read a syllabus and calculate your grade

★ How to know when your grade requires you speak to your instructor or your counselor

★ What to do when you're failing a class

★ When to recognize that you need a tutor or academic support

★ What consequences to expect if there are problems from family members

★ The consequences of missing an appointment

★ What to do if you get lost on campus

★ How to contact your instructors

★ What to do if you are bullied or see someone bullied

★ What to do if you are late to class.

The list can be different for each student, but it's best for them to anticipate as much as possible ahead of time to make things easier. Working with college staff can also help in adding things to the list that the student may have missed.

I ended the above list with "What to do if you are late to class." Some of my students are concerned about being late to class mostly because they do not want to draw attention to themselves as they walk into a classroom. I remember one in particular, Maria. Many of Maria's classes were in a program where courses only met once a week for 2.5 hours. One week there was horrible traffic, and she ended up coming to campus five minutes after the class had already started. While most students would then probably find the first parking spot available and run into class as quickly as they could, she was afraid to leave her car. She stayed in her car paralyzed with fear the entire class time, and then never reached out to anyone afterward, out of embarrassment. As a result, she missed out on a significant amount of class time that was difficult to make up. While we like to believe students will always make it on time to every single class session, the inevitable and unexpected can happen, and any student will likely be late to class once in a while. Make sure to have a discussion on what to do when this happens.

Sometimes I have to remind myself as a therapist that the words I might use to describe symptoms are not always the ones that students identify with. For example, I might ask a student, "What causes you anxiety?" or "What stresses you out?" and they may not connect with these vague statements. While stress and anxiety strike a chord for many of us, often for those on the spectrum these concepts of stress, anxiety, or broadly labeled mental health symptoms are not fully defined. Instead, I try to focus on using language that's more directly connected to the related thought patterns. For example, "Are there things about school that you find yourself thinking about all the time?" or "What are the things about school you think will cause you the most difficulty right now?" can be useful questions.

Some students can also struggle with *catastrophizing*, or taking a fear and moving it to a case scenario so awful the consequences become unrealistic. Let's go back to the example of my student who stayed in her car after arriving on campus five minutes late. First, she may have thought that her late arrival would upset the instructor, who would then lower her letter grade. And also, the angry instructor might make fun of her, resulting in not only the lower grade, but also her fellow students making fun of her. That concern led to the idea that her parents would find out she had upset everyone, and they would get so angry they would pull her out of school entirely and cut off her access to technology. Having been forced to drop out of school, with no access to technology, she would have a horrible life.

While it's easy to step away from this type of situation and recognize that this chain of events would never occur, it's a far different thing to be in the moment itself, experiencing it and living it. Imagine the degree of fear and anxiety this thought process would cause. And can you imagine if this string of fears unfurled whenever the unexpected occurred, and how exhausting life would be in that case? It's very important to assess not only a person's autism, but also their coping mechanisms, ways to handle the unexpected and the anxiety that comes with it. By overlooking the possibility of such stymieing events, we put students at a great disadvantage.

Chapter 5

Technology

Our Friend and Enemy

Without a doubt the greatest threat and benefit to students on the autism spectrum today is technology. Certainly, one need not think long to see the advantages it provides. Email communication can make asking questions and sharing information easier, websites deliver a range of helpful research and clarifying information, video games can serve as a great outlet for escape and entertainment when one's work is done, social media keeps us connected to one another in a way that never seemed possible just generations previously, and the breakthroughs in medicine, including improvements in how we treat mental illness and address physiological issues, are among the greatest discoveries of the last century. Without a doubt, technology has a vital role in our society and is here to stay.

But there are also ways technology can be abused. Like any other means of escapism (drinking, drugs, avoidance, sex, etc.), technology can be addictive and dangerous. Video gaming in particular can be a trap for many of my students. Likewise, social media brings its own addictive challenges and issues. So let's talk a little more about these two prevailing forces in our culture, and go over strategies you can use to avoid them becoming a serious problem.

The speed and complexity video games have developed over the last ten years has been nothing short of amazing. We can now game not only with an anonymous computer, but also with our friends on the couch, our friends online on the other side of town, and even with strangers on the other side of the world. The thought of this reach is very exciting. With each game there can be entire microcosms of complexities that require video game controllers with over ten buttons each on them and endless combinations to produce results. We know from previous discussion that these worlds of information bounded in an artificial environment can be very compelling to a spectrum adult. It's like being Lewis and Clark journeying to the West Coast for the first time—endless territories to explore and people to meet! And the great thing about video game worlds is their predictability. We know that by pressing B+A+Z we can make our hero shoot a fireball or perform a jump attack. By hitting X over and over quickly we can generate a funny comment, and by shaking the remote we can make the entire world itself shake in excitement. And, thanks to internet connectivity, once we discover all these capabilities, we can show them off to our friends, or even impress strangers all around the world with our gaming prowess. It becomes a source of confidence and pride, *along with* escaping all the stresses of the outside world.

The gaming industry has gotten very smart about cashing in on the enticements of the gaming experience. For example, one of the video games many of my spectrum students currently love, Super Smash Bros. for the Wii U, costs anywhere from $60 to $80 for the base video game, plus smaller fees to add additional characters to their game— characters that almost everyone identifies with and loves. And then, once you have the characters, you can pay an additional fee on top of that for them to perform specialized moves or make funny sound effects. I have had many a student tell me they've already invested over $150 on a single video game, and still have plans for adding to it in the future!

I do not mean to say that video games should not have a role in my students' lives. On the contrary, games can be an important outlet for decreasing stress, relaxing, and temporarily escaping the outside world. To deny a person this activity cold turkey would seem unfair, and having worked with parents and students where it was cut off entirely, I can say that the outcome is rarely positive. An interesting side note—when I asked Temple Grandin (whom I discuss in a later chapter) what she considered the single greatest threat to young adults on the spectrum today, she said video games, due to their addictive nature!

The key, however, as with any addictive substance, is to help students develop boundaries and learn how to control their use of it. I'm a big fan of structured leisure time in set amounts. Allowing students an hour or two per day to go gaming is a reasonable expectation as long as there is a clearly defined starting time and ending time. I think times are better than amounts because amounts can get blurred. It's better to say, for example, someone can game from 3 to 5 pm than for two hours because by agreeing on a time it creates structure, just like a job or a class, that can be anticipated and clearly measured.

Ideally the young adult uses video game systems rather than the internet to game. Stand-alone systems can easily be unplugged from the wall, and moved to another location if necessary, should the person refuse to turn the system off. Online gaming like World of Warcraft and Hearthstone, however, can be more dangerous in that a person can easily jump to gaming and fun websites on a computer during homework time and focus more on gaming than finishing work. For children who are online gamers, I highly recommend parents agreeing with their children to review their browsing history to make sure there is no deviation from academic work.

Once there is firm agreement on the rules for gaming (particularly when it is and isn't allowed), parents need to make sure they follow this plan. As soon as the lines begin to be blurred ("you've had a hard day today, you can have an extra hour"), parents teach the lesson that gaming is a negotiable commodity. This flexibility will lead to arguments and frustration in the future. The clearer cut things can be, the better.

Social media can be another area of confusion and difficulty. Networks like Facebook, Instagram, and Twitter are in their infancy in terms of our understanding of their social effects within our larger world culture, and can be an area of confusion for almost all college students. Video games also frequently have their own social media elements where a person can chat while playing, or observe others gaming while chatting with them. For many spectrum adults, these exchanges can serve as an important part of socialization.

I remember one student explaining to me why online chatting was more enjoyable than in-person conversations: "When you talk to someone in person, there's so much to deal with. There's all the facial expression things, all the background noise, and you don't have any time to think about what to say. Online, there's none of this, no body language, nuances, or hidden messages, and you can think a minute before you type something. It's a more natural way for me to communicate." This view makes sense. In a world of sensory overload in every direction, the controlled world of the internet can be an oasis.

Likewise, as gaming plays an important role for many adults, so does social media. Again, the key similarity goes back to structure. Set times should be created when these things are okay to do and that schedule should be kept as regular as possible. Also, remember that it is rare for anyone to need a smartphone to do homework! Encourage parents to encourage their children to remove the phone entirely from the study situation, unless absolutely necessary. The temptations to drift off path are just too great, particularly with the phone issuing constant updates and alerts.

Another potentially problematic element of social media relates to safety. While it goes without saying people should never share their birthdate, credit card number, social security number, or any other personal information online, along with any kind of photographs with nudity of any sort, this can be a confusing area when the person on the other side of the computer is up to no good. I've had students share topless photos, bottomless photos, or their credit card numbers because the other person told them they were their boyfriend/ girlfriend and someone they could trust. Periodically reiterate the potential dangers of sharing this kind of information, and make sure your student understands no romantic partner would ever expect this kind of information to be shared.

On a different topic related to technology, more and more colleges are offering online instruction as an option for college. Online classes can serve a wonderful purpose—they allow people with significant disabilities, working adults, people in remote areas, and countless other groups an opportunity to get an education when otherwise it might not be possible. Sometimes parents will ask me if I think online classes might be a good solution for their child. In a lot of ways on the surface it makes sense—their child gravitates towards technology, it eliminates all the stresses of being in a classroom environment, it takes away the stresses of transportation, etc. It sounds perfect!

For some students, online schooling can be a good option. Certainly, for those students who also struggle significantly with anxiety, or have difficulty focusing in a classroom environment, conventional school can be next to impossible, and the internet can be a viable pathway to an education. For most students, however, the disadvantages outweigh the benefits. There are the traps we've discussed previously—it's too easy to jump to distracting websites; there is a lack of structure around how work is to be done; and an online school can increase social isolation. If a student is adamant about trying it, I always attempt to negotiate a happy medium in which they split their time for their first semester, taking one class online and one in a classroom to compare the two. More often than not I find students miss numerous deadlines for the online course until it is too late to make up the work, and a lot of money ends up getting wasted as a result.

In conclusion, we should talk as openly about technology as about alcohol, drugs, and sex. It is a welcome part of our society that makes connectivity easier but can also lead to negative consequences. Openness and honesty are the keys to using it intelligently. Not only do smart behaviors around technology make college go more smoothly, they also become vital when the student transitions to the work world—better for these lessons to be learned now rather than once they are in a job they've worked very hard to attain.

Chapter 6

Relationships

From Friendships to Dating to Sex

One of the more obvious, yet ignored, transitions that we forget about are all the relationship issues that come with adulthood. Remember, this young person is indeed now an adult and will be treated as such. In fact, if you know much of higher education law, then you've probably already heard about a particular law called FERPA, or the Federal Educational Release of Privacy Act. It states that anyone 18 years of age or older is legally considered an adult, so information regarding their grades, financial aid, attendance, medical records, or almost anything cannot be released without the student's written permission. This right to privacy is taken very seriously. For example, if a parent emails an instructor asking if their child is attending class, the teacher may very well not write back at all, or respond that the information cannot be shared without the child's written consent.

As a therapist working with adults on the autism spectrum for many years now, I have learned that while philosophically I agree this is an important law to have in place, there are times when parental involvement is important. It's hard to say how and when, because I tend to look at things on a case-by-case basis, but I certainly recommend that families talk about FERPA and the level of parental involvement early on. And make sure it's an honest and open talk.

If a student is adamant that parental involvement is intrusive, forcing the matter will probably not reap much benefit for anyone involved. An interesting detail about FERPA is that students can give or revoke their FERPA rights at any time. I remember one mother who forced her son to go to the college's records office to sign the release of information form. "If I'm paying your tuition, I need to know everything that's going on!" she told him. Sure enough, he signed it, and sure enough, the next day, when his mother wasn't around, he revoked it. Imagine how comfortable the conversation was the next day when his mom called me to find out whether he had come to class that day, and I had to say that I couldn't tell her. Parents forcing their way in just doesn't work, and even if they're successful, most college students are clever enough to find ways to get around the system.

Now back to relationships. As we've established, this "child" is now an adult. As such, they may want to have closer friendships, dating relationships, and most probably are even a little curious and also interested in sex. For parents reading this and fearing this chapter is turning into a sex education lesson; it isn't. But if they think their beloved child Tommy or Tammy, regardless of disability or functioning level, doesn't think about sex from time to time as an 18-year-old with hormones bouncing in every direction, they are truly deluding themselves!

The student's high school should have provided some coursework on social education, but whether it did or didn't, parents should have a conversation about some of the social rules that come with establishing friendships. If parents have not had this conversation, you may need to have this instead. For example, it's perfectly normal to ask a fellow classmate to go out for coffee in person or by email once, but it's not okay to send ten different emails the same day asking this question. Also, it's okay to talk with a new person outside of the classroom, but probably not a good idea to follow that new acquaintance around for 20 minutes and then work up the courage to ask that person for coffee while in the library. Talk about how there is a time and a place for conversations to occur, and how to recognize if a person is interested or not in becoming a friend.

The same guidelines apply to romantic relationships. I've had students who have wanted to ask a fellow classmate out on a date and who really struggle with popping the question. Let's be honest, regardless of disability, this is something that was hard for most of us at that age. Encourage role-playing, and if a student isn't comfortable talking about relationships with you, encourage him or her to seek out someone they trust, like a family friend, college counselor, or other staff person at the institution.

I have found some of the students I work with tend toward obsessive-compulsive communication methods. This is especially true with social media and email, which facilitate sending emails/texts/messages over and over again, sometimes never getting a response, leading to great frustration and anxiety. Encourage students to talk about the frequency of communications with a specific person, and how often that person communicates in return. The content itself is none of your business, but helping the student understand that quantity does not equate with quality can be helpful. If you find this kind of over-communicating does become problematic with the person you are working with, you should take steps right away. Obsessive communication, although innocent to you, can be perceived very differently by someone else. And remember, this person is now an adult, so uninvited excessive communication can also lead to legal repercussions. Clear, open communication is critical.

Of course, in most cases a student's communication with classmates is very healthy and ordinary. Fortunately, many experience what I call the "Like Me" phenomenon when they get to college. In high school, they may have known a few people on the spectrum, or met others with similar personalities to their own, but because of the size and diversity of the institution, college can yield a whole host of friends with similar interests. I always find new discovery of a sense of community encouraging and wonderful—it's one of the reasons I started the Autismerica organization that I talk about in Chapter 10, to help encourage it even further. There's something so great about finding friends who truly understand your way of seeing the world and other people.

This "Like Me" reaction can be problematic, too, however. For example, on my campus there is a lounge where many of the children I'd call spectrum students and those with similar personalities hang out. They play card games like Magic and Yu-Gi-Oh!, online games like World of Warcraft and Hearthstone, and share comics of Manga or superheroes. Some have such a wonderful time connecting with fellow classmates they lose track of time and end up missing class. Or they ignore their studies and homework so they can hang out over the weekend playing Dungeons and Dragons and Axis and Allies with their new friends. Encourage students to make connections with others, but always make sure the work is being done and the agreement on a regulated amount of time for work is being honored.

Make sure students have a responsible and sex-educated person to talk with about sex as well. Ideally this person would be a parent, but if not, encourage students to seek out others who are informed and articulate, such as counselors, other trusted family members, or medical professionals.

Here are some of the more commonly asked questions and comments about sex that I hear from students:

★ How much masturbation is too much? Will it hurt me?

★ Does oral sex mean I've lost my virginity?

★ Will condoms prevent pregnancy?

★ My boyfriend wants me to Snapchat him a picture with my top off. Is this okay?

★ I think I might be gay but I'm not sure.

★ How do I get birth control?

★ Can I get an STD from kissing?

★ What does it feel like? Does it hurt?

★ If he pulls out, I won't get pregnant, right?

★ What does a penis/vagina look like?

★ Am I asexual since I don't want to have sex yet?

★ How do I know if I am bisexual?

Now obviously, I get these questions on a case-by-case basis. Not every student is curious about these things, and many, as a result of their autism, view actual sexual intercourse as something they have no interest in trying for some time. But if a student has these kinds of questions, encourage the conversation, with you or someone else they trust.

One of my favorite movies out there on the topic of Asperger's and adult relationships is the film *Adam* (2009). For most of his life Adam has relied on his father to connect him to the outside world. When the story begins, his father has died, and Adam must now go it alone. He is intellectually a very bright computer programmer but struggles with all the classical issues people on the Asperger's side of the spectrum can struggle with—organization, communication, time management, etc. In the film, he eventually does get a job and starts dating a woman who is not on the autism spectrum, and he learns a lot about relationships along the way. It's a great movie to watch, as it deals with aspects of adulthood and relationships in a very true and authentic manner. It can lead to a nice discussion afterward, making the transition to these various topics a little less awkward.

Above all, encourage students to seek out interactions in whatever ways they most enjoy, and always with balance. Electronic communications like Facebook, Twitter, etc. can be great, in moderation. In-person communication, whether via gaming or talking, can be wonderful, too. Try to encourage variety and balance, and successful relationships will follow.

Chapter 7

Career Exploration and Life After College

What's Next?

The question of what to do *after* college is one that many parents and students on the spectrum don't consider as much as they should. This lack of post-educational planning makes sense: from the first day a person is diagnosed, which is normally in a school setting, the goal becomes doing everything possible to make that school experience a successful one. From IEP meetings to accommodations planning to graduation petitions, the road can seem endless. But the day will come for parents when a college application asks their child to fill in a box regarding an intended major, and then another one will follow sooner than expected: that walk across the stage to receive an associate's, bachelor's, or master's degree, maybe even a doctorate, and then the question: "Now what?"

To start, it's never too early to begin career exploration. I encourage this process to begin in high school. Students change their intended area of study all the time, which is fine, but starting the process early on plants the seed that a career is the ultimate goal. There are lots of great career exploration inventories for help with brainstorming ideas. The Strong Interest Inventory, Self-Directed-Search (SDS), and California Occupational Preference Survey (COPS) are some of my personal favorites, but there are other instruments out there as well. I recommend that if you do use career exploration tools, use those that are interest-based rather than personality-based, such as the Myers-Briggs Type Indicator, which is more of a personality inventory. I find the personality tools are geared toward the general population, which, as a result, only include a fraction of people on the spectrum. Taking into account the uniqueness of personality that often accompanies adults on the spectrum, such tests will yield less accurate results for your student.

For many young adults, technology becomes a first area of consideration. Fields like computer programming, networking, and computer repair are hands-on occupations that involve technology and do not require complex social interaction. For those students who are also good at math, fields like engineering science, actuarial science, or experimental psychology can be possibilities. For those exceptional at drawing or writing, animation and graphic design are worth considering.

But what about young adults who aren't techies? Maybe they are more interested in studying volumes of Japanese cartoon anime or collecting train timetables from around the world. How do you turn such unique interests into occupational exploration? First, you obviously want to think about careers that are directly connected to those personal interests. If they love animation, can they find work in either creating it or writing it? For those interested in trains, is there work in transportation? Direct links are great whenever possible.

But maybe those direct links don't exist, or it isn't realistic to expect the area of interest to lead to a job. In this case, looking at transferable skills and talents that come from those areas of personal interest can be a good starting point. If a student has an ability to organize information to a great level of detail, you might look into library technology, which requires such skills. If a student loves to sing and listens to music all the time, sound engineering is a growing field that combines technology and music, and can lead to all kinds of musical creations.

Another important point: always make sure you're looking at occupational data involving these careers as well. Creative career ideas are all well and good, but if at the end of a student's studies the ideas can't become a real occupation, a lot of effort has been invested for nothing. The government maintains the website Occupational

Outlook Handbook,[1] which provides current employment statistics by state for almost every occupation you can think of. Not to push community colleges too much, but one of the many things I like about them is that for a school to maintain its accreditation for an occupational program, it needs to have at least a decent employability rate for its graduates. So almost any major at a community college has great potential for the future.

What if after all this exploration and effort nothing comes to fruition? Certainly, many of the first year college students I work with are unsure how they are going to become employed, but in those cases, I recommend using the first year of studies as a chance to experiment with different subjects. Almost any undergraduate degree, whether an associate's or bachelor's degree, allows the student to have a certain amount of elective credit in conjunction with almost any major. It is much better to engage in this experimentation early on than to realize much later that something you thought would be great is not the right major after all.

Sometimes advisors will push students to secure all their broad-based requirements for their major before doing anything else. (We call these the general education requirements—things like English composition, math, science, and communications.) This approach is sound; the sooner all these less interesting but necessary requirements are out of the way, the sooner the student can focus on an intended major. For students who know what they want to do for a major, this advising style makes perfect sense. For undecided students, however, taking a lot of general education courses before they have a sense of direction only delays necessary experimentation. Thus, for the typical student attending full-time, I encourage only one or two general education classes, and then as many elective courses as possible, to allow for dabbling in different areas.

In terms of length of study, we are seeing the model for the traditional associate's degree shift from two years to three, and the model for a bachelor's degree pushing five years. I advocate moving slower if finances allow. Granted, sometimes the cost of university

---

1   See www.bls.gov/ooh/

attendance or of state grant-funded programs makes it impossible to extend enrollment, but added semesters often allow students to add an internship near the end of their studies, which can be crucial to success after college.

Internships used to be a standard requirement of almost any program in higher education. They allow the student to attain practical experience in a professional setting, solidifying the area of study as a future career match and giving the student some practical work experience to assist in finding a job after graduation. More and more, however, I see academic programs have pushed out internship requirements, now making it an option, but not necessarily a requirement for graduation. This change is unfortunate. To me, the internship for a spectrum adult is one of the single most important experiences of their college career. It helps build confidence and expectations, and gives the student that foot in the door that might otherwise not be possible. On top of that, colleges have important services for a person with a disability—the disability accommodations office, counseling center, and academic advisors all at the student's disposal to troubleshoot problems and lend support for that critical first step.

Once a student has chosen a major and has some degree of confidence in it, start talking about internships, even if they are studying an area that requires obvious future graduate work, such as psychology or medicine. While in these areas the internship is probably less directly connected to ultimate employment, given accreditation issues, it still gives the student a chance to build some professional experience, attain some positive work references, and further confirm that the area of study is indeed a good career match.

Speaking of internships, if a student is still undecided after a couple years of college, but you both feel some practical experience would be helpful, there are some more broad-based internship programs that are useful for any major. One of my favorite opportunities is the Disney internship program (and no, I'm not getting any kickbacks for sharing this opinion). Students from all around the country can intern at Disney for either a six- or nine-month period. The jobs themselves are mostly menial—janitorial, food service, greeting, ticket taking, etc.—but the student gets a whole host of skills from the experience.

The Disney program provides housing for each employee, which the student will share with three roommates. It also provides food, free access to the parks, and a small budget for outside living expenses and transportation. Students establish skills of independent living, having roommates (which is often a probable reality for their futures), managing money, and again, building practical work experience they can one day use to market themselves. Another perk: students who successfully finish the program with positive reviews gain a connection to many of the larger companies within Disney, such as Pixar, ESPN, and ABC television.

So we've put a lot of energy into talking about career exploration; I'd now like to change direction and talk about the other large focus of this chapter, the transition out of higher education and into the Real World. This, too, is a major step that can be riddled with all kinds of fears and apprehensions. So what are some of things that can be done in the last year of college to make this as smooth as possible?

We've already talked about internships, and I cannot reiterate enough how much I believe in internships for personal and professional development. Another important area, however, is interviewing skills. I tell students that while we live in a world where laws like the Americans with Disabilities Act (ADA) and related discrimination laws are set up to protect adults with disabilities from discrimination, the reality is that ugliness exists and can be truly pernicious. Up to this point of transition out of college and into the work world, the student has often had parents as advocates, as well as high school or college staff to help drive the point home that this person is capable of almost anything, with the proper services in place. But everyone is on his or her own in the job market. When young adults are just beginning to learn how to self-advocate and market themselves, they can encounter a lot of trouble if there isn't some practice and discussion ahead of time.

Most colleges have a career services center that can help. They are staffed with people who will assist with writing resumes and looking for jobs. They even set up and conduct mock interviews. I am a *huge* fan of mock interviews. Technology today makes it extremely easy to videotape them, and I recommend doing so and then reviewing the tapes with people the student trusts for honest feedback and advice. By the way, this is not a time to sugarcoat feedback if the student interviews horribly. Trust me, most future employers will not look at this person in as kind a light as you, as the professional counselor. Be critical. Better yet, ask outsiders to review the tapes, as they can be even more critical, in ways that will benefit the student.

Repeat this interview process over and over. I tell spectrum students who struggle with communication that they should have at least ten different mock interviews before going into the first real one. The learning that comes from these experiences is incredibly important. And try to vary the personalities of the people doing the mock interviews as much as possible. Look for all types. The more unexpected the interview can be, the better. It helps teach the lesson that the interview will be one of the most unpredictable experiences a person has in a career; preparation for almost any question will be key to success, because questions in interviews vary more than most students expect.

Students often ask me when in the process of the job search they should share the accommodation needs connected to their disability. From a legal perspective, it is highly recommended that nothing about a person's disability should be shared in the initial interview (and should not be brought up by the interviewer either), and only after the job offer has been made should a conversation about needs centered round accommodation take place. It's also recommended practice for spectrum adults that even if they don't think they will require any accommodations on the job, they should share information, so if a communication breakdown or organizational issue ever arises, they've been proactive in letting their employer know they are on the spectrum.

"What if I tell an employer about myself and then they treat me differently or revoke the job offer?" students will ask me. Well, I have a couple things to say in response to this. First, unfortunately, we do live in a world where people can disguise their actions and thus discriminate without it ever looking like they did so. So yes, it's possible the job won't come through, and I acknowledge that. But then I ask the student if this really were to be the case, would they want to work for them anyway? They might fall under the radar upon being hired, but the first time a misunderstanding occurs, there will probably be a lack of patience and understanding on the employer's part. Second, employers want a job placement to be successful just as much as the people applying for the job. Everybody wants a win-win when it comes to hiring someone. It's in both the student's and the employer's best interests to get everything out on the table so discussion can occur to make the job placement successful.

Remember that there are state services that can also help with employment. In Chapter 3, I discussed vocational rehabilitation—a state-by-state government agency that helps people with disabilities find jobs. These agencies often have access to state positions that are not as extensively marketed on traditional employment websites and venues. Another benefit of state services can be access to job coaches and scouts who help people on the spectrum look for employment, and once they get a job, accompany them for the first few weeks to serve as an intermediary between the employer and the person with a disability, to address any issues that might arise. It's an additional support that is free of charge to help new jobholders be successful. Incidentally, once a person finds a job, while his or her file might be closed in that moment, people on the spectrum can always choose to have their services reinstated should they need to find a different job or their career aspirations change—it isn't a one-time placement service.

So, in conclusion, the transition to the Real World need not be as scary and horrible as one might think. Rather, it is yet another change that, with planning and practice, can lead to independence, confidence, and freedom. As I type this, I'm grinning. I can imagine parents reading this chapter, raising their eyebrows, and thinking, "Oh, yeah?" And my response is, "Yes!" I've done this work long enough to know the list of unexpected hiccups can seem never-ending at times. But please remember: always look forward, maintain connections, and seek out expertise whenever needed. Good luck!

Chapter 8

Regarding Developmental and Intellectual Disabilities

Used as a catch-all by many different disability groups, the term *developmental disability* can be quite subjective in its interpretation. To some people, autism itself is a developmental disability. In its literal sense, a developmental disability is "a group of conditions due to an impairment in physical, learning, language, or behavior areas."[1] By this definition, autism would qualify as a disability.

So far, I have written a lot about success for children on the spectrum who are of average intellectual functioning ranges, meaning that a traditional college experience is possible with the right services and accommodations. So, for the purposes of this chapter, I'd like to address another important group that is too often overlooked—students who are of a level of intellectual or psychosocial functioning that makes pursuing a college-level degree unrealistic. I'm going to talk about the idea of developmental disabilities in its application to young adults who are in the borderline intellectual functioning to moderately intellectually disabled categories. Many high school and community college students on the autism spectrum fall into this category—dually diagnosed into both groups of autism *and* lower intellectual functioning—and there is very little written about and for them in regard to success in adulthood.

This is the group among all of those I work with that most often falls through the cracks in terms of services available to adults, and colleges' responses to them. In many ways, they don't fall into any

---

1   See www.cdc.gov/ncbddd/autism/facts.html

category within the traditional educational and service delivery models, but theirs is a large and growing group that desperately needs services and training.

From a higher education perspective, there are not many programs offered at universities or even community colleges. While obviously this population would not be one for baccalaureate programs at university level, community colleges should certainly be responding to their needs. Still, very few programs in the country are offered at community college level, and even when they are, in most cases they are noncredit offerings, with little standards and ineligible for financial aid.

Part of this problem exists on the larger scale of educational elitism. Every level lacks adequate training programs and resources. For example, in recent years, Congress added an additional requirement that students who are on financial aid must receive a high school diploma. And note, this must be a full-fledged diploma, not a modified one, which is often offered to students with developmental intellectual delays. Thus, from the highest levels comes the message that this group does not belong in higher education.

On the state level, accrediting agencies also often push back on community colleges that offer programs for students with developmental delays. It is next to impossible in most states to get any for-credit coursework accredited for this group. The classic argument concerns academic rigor: "How can coursework geared toward a person of low intellectual functioning possibly have any academic rigor and challenge?" faculty will say. Yet, what is academic rigor? Many faculty who question the validity of accredited courses for students with disabilities define academic rigor as the type of demonstrated learning that can only happen through a paper or written examination. But remember, there are other subjects in higher education that do not have this type of evaluation and that are more skills-based, and these classes are approved. For example, physical education, music, and art are all important subjects in higher education, but students traditionally show proficiency by demonstrating a skill like playing an instrument or performing a physical feat. This type of skill-based learning is considered valid in the college model, so why can't colleges do the same for students on the spectrum? *Why is one group allowed certification and one not?*

What is the real reason why many community colleges don't offer appropriate coursework to students with developmental limitations? The answer, I suspect, relates to intellectual elitism. Community colleges often pride themselves more on the "college" part of their identity than on "community," and fear how other students will react to seeing students with developmental delays on their college campuses. Many community colleges already operate with the fear of being a joke in the public eye—comedians will often make jokes about community college students, implying they are failures who could not make it in the traditional university model, and seeing students with intellectual delays only emphasizes the stereotypes. While these beliefs may indeed be out there, *they are completely unfounded.* Rather, community colleges serve one of the most important needs of towns and cities across the country—training students for both occupations and future university studies in an affordable, service-oriented way. Given the mission of community colleges to serve all people in the community, I'm always surprised by how few offer classes for students with developmental disabilities.

One group, disturbingly, that has joined the chorus criticizing the lack of community college services are for-profit universities and programs. In some cases, these institutions do a wonderful job training students for the future by offering vocational coursework and internship opportunities, but they typically charge exorbitant tuition fees. I have met with parents who have taken out second mortgages on their homes to pay for their children to be in these programs, believing there is no other option for their children's futures. I find this hardship on families very upsetting and disappointing. Also remember that these programs are rarely, if ever, FAFSA/financial aid-eligible because of the requirements of high school graduation.

Still, families might be in a financial situation where they can afford such a program, or they are willing to work to earn the extra money to make this training available to their child. Should they go for it? Before signing up, I encourage the family to inspect the program carefully. They should ask about the degree of education of the trainers and their level of experience. It is a reasonable expectation that the director of a program has at least a master's degree in some area of special education or rehabilitation counselor education, and the teachers should all have at least bachelor's degrees in their respective disciplines or a degree in special education. There are no federal requirements for standardization of these types of for-profit programs, so almost anyone can teach them. If a person is paying the tuition of a university for education, it is reasonable for them to expect faculty with a comparable level of training and education.

Parents should also ask how many graduates are successfully placed in jobs, and where they are placed. Are they job placements that students want, or jobs that they could have gotten anyway, without attending the university or training program in the first place? Also, are internships offered? If not, this is a major red flag. As with any other university program, an internship is a critical way to earn job experience and learn skills. If the program is not seeking internships for its students, what can be expected in terms of job placement upon graduation? Parents should scrutinize the program very carefully before signing off on that loan to pay for it.

So, if you are working with a family with such a young adult of lower intellectual functioning, what do you do if there aren't any colleges or universities in the area offering appropriate coursework? Or maybe there is such a school nearby, but the program is not affordable? Start by looking at all training programs in your area in depth, beginning with the community college. Call that school's disability services office (every school is required to have one), and ask to speak with a service provider there. Serving students with developmental disabilities is an area near and dear to most providers' hearts, and they will typically share the sentiment that this is an often-ignored group of students. They will be able to tell you whether there are any academic programs that will realistically prepare young adults for the future, and will know the level of intellectual functioning required for a student to be successful. If there are appropriate course offerings, set up a meeting with the student's family for all of them to work together in determining what the offerings are, and if any of these relate to the interests of the young adult.

If there are no realistic offerings at the college, shift your focus to vocational rehabilitation. As mentioned in Chapter 3, vocational rehabilitation is a state-by-state federally funded program that offers assistance to people with disabilities in finding employment. They may have access to different training programs that can also prepare children for the future in the form of specialized training. For example, in Chicago, there is a program called Asperitech, which specifically recruits adults on the autism spectrum regardless of functioning level for employment opportunities. The local vocational rehabilitation office might have information for similar programs to help with training.

If a family hits dead-ends with both community college and vocational rehabilitation, they—and you—still shouldn't be afraid to push the system. Both options should be offering well-developed services. Ask college administrators why they choose to ignore this group, ask to have a student's case transferred to another rehabilitation counselor should you feel the person they've been working with isn't committed to helping meet the needs of that person (something students are legally allowed to do), and don't be afraid to go all the way to the top of both organizations should you find that nothing is happening. A call to the branch manager of the Department of Human Services or the office of the community college president can do wonders. In many cases, these are the people with the true power to take action on a larger scale, and may not even be aware of the lack of services out there. Never be afraid to advocate, not only for the person you are working with, but also for the thousands more in your community who are underserved!

In the meantime, however, what if there are no community college programs with offerings applicable, and the state-provided employment services for people with disabilities in your area only offer minimal services and/or training to help young adults—then what do you do? The next step is to advise parents to talk with other parents.

Truly, nobody knows more about services and community offerings than parents themselves, and why wouldn't they? Their children and their futures are their top priorities. Trying to network with other parents through local high schools, or through recreational groups like Special Olympics, which are offered almost everywhere, or trying to get an email for a Facebook group started: these are simple ways to connect with even the busiest of parents to share resources and information.

There is a certain beauty to parents working together. For example, here in Chicago, there is a wonderful program called We Grow Dreams (www.wegrowdreams.org). This is a group of parents with children who have developmental disabilities, parents who wanted to create an opportunity for their children to be able to work and participate, to share their skills with the world. They purchased a plot of land and pooled all their money to hire farmers to work with their children in cultivating the land and growing a variety of fruit and vegetables to sell for profit while giving each child a job. Parents pay a small stake for their children to participate. The program has been a wonderful success.

Another question I sometimes get regarding students with intellectual limitations is applying for social security/disability. If a family has exhausted every possibility and success still eludes them, I recommend that they consider this option for their child's financial future. Sadly, the process has become a difficult one due to some (note, only some) people who have tried to scam the system to receive SSI (Supplemental Security Income) without meeting the criteria. Because of this issue, the processing time alone normally takes over a year, and sadly, I have rarely seen anyone, even families dealing with the most severe of disabling conditions, be successful without hiring an attorney for representation. Again, networking with parents for referrals of attorneys can be essential—and don't trust the lawyers advertising on television. They often lead to a dead end, and cost a lot of money in the process.

As frustrating as the process can be, families must plan for their child's future. Their staying at home doing nothing is the worst thing possible. Even if the family is successful in attaining social security/disability, work should still be sought, even on a volunteer basis, to help the young adult in creating a sense of meaning and self-worth. *Leaving a child at home every day is the worst thing that can happen.* Remember, as difficult as financial security is to think about, most children outlive their parents, and when parents are gone, the person they are left to reside with, if anyone, will probably not provide the degree of devotion and attention that parents themselves have provided for years, even if that person is trustworthy.

Encourage families to address their child's future early with the questions, "What if the parent (and/or their significant other) were killed tomorrow in a car crash? Would the services be in place, and the people on call to assist them? What would happen?" Encourage families to make certain a trust is in place, a will is written, and they've talked to those that parents wish to be involved in their child's future. Learning skills of independent living is a must—can they do their own laundry? Feed themselves? Pay bills? They must be prepared as much as possible for the future.

Addressing all of these concerns is certainly overwhelming. Incredibly so. But remember, no one is alone in the process. Hundreds of thousands of parents across the country struggle with similar issues every day. Encourage parents to do everything they can to connect with others in similar situations. They could use social media, form parent groups, put up fliers, and always reach out, no matter how busy things get. I meet many parents who describe their frustrations and disappointments and feel they are the only ones in the world experiencing such things. Connecting with others not only makes parents feel more empowered, but it can also be deeply therapeutic.

Chapter 9

What Makes a Good Counselor?

I've been a therapist for about 20 years and have learned a lot from a variety of experiences, including my mistakes. A student interviewed me once for a paper she was writing for a human services course, and she asked me, "What's your counseling philosophy?" I was surprised how difficult a question it was for me to answer. In thinking about it, however, I see my approach as one that draws from many different categories.

Above all else, I consider myself a person-centered therapist. Also known as Rogerian therapy, person-centered therapy focuses on building relationships and rapport with individual clients so they feel safe and open to talk about anything that is on their minds. The founder of this approach, Carl Rogers, was a therapist who worked in Chicago during the 1950s and 1960s. Rogers emphasized the importance of trust and honesty, and I have found forging those bonds absolutely critical in my work. If a person doesn't feel safe, it's hard to move forward.

Rogerian therapy is particularly relevant to working with today's Millennials and Generation Z students. They use technology as their primary driver to communicate and interact with one another; they value connectedness, but of a fairly shallow variety; and, contrary to popular opinion, they are extremely hard workers. As a result of a continual outpouring of information and their access to it, however, today's emerging adults can become rather jaded and distrustful.

In addition, there are the experiences that accompany being a student in today's high school environment. The IEP/IDEA

(Individuals with Disabilities Education Act) process emphasizes identification, so even though every effort is made to protect identity, almost any student will tell you that their classmates knew who was on an IEP, and most resent that the information was public. When we look at the research, we see only about half of new college students self-identify as having a disability and seek out services. When I meet with a new student I can tell within minutes whether I will see that student again very soon, or not for a long time (typically after things have fallen apart). Those who want to run, preferring not to meet with me at any time, are usually dragged in by their parents, whereas those seeking services actively participate in the discussion.

Their reluctance to embrace working with me is no surprise, and certainly understandable. If we look back, past the nostalgia, we realize that our teens were in many ways some of the most difficult years of our lives. Relationships and social status are at the forefront, and in this technological age of easily shared information, there are no secrets. The vulnerability students must feel coming into college and their uncertainty about what to expect has got to be unsettling. Yet there is an enticing flip side: college represents a fresh start.

So, a humanistic or person-centered approach is critical. These students often feel misunderstood by the current secondary education system, particularly its predilection for labels and paperwork, and this faulty labeling is coupled with a natural instinct among most teens to distrust the views of older adults. Because autism entails such a broad spectrum of functioning, students may struggle with their identity and how it fits with their diagnosis. They may see lower-functioning students struggling with learning basic concepts and feel frustrated because they don't identify with those other students, and they may see higher-functioning students performing advanced trigonometry and not identify with them either. Students can easily feel lost in today's system. They will often say that ours is a different generation, and we don't understand what it's like to be young today, and they're right. Quite honestly, I don't know if I would survive puberty if I had to do it all over again in this era of social media, overabundance of false information online, and seemingly endless ways to get into trouble by the negative influences of drugs, alcohol, and dangerous substances.

So how do we, as counselors, establish a relationship with students? We make some respectful assumptions. We assume that although we are well trained in our discipline, we cannot possibly understand what it is like to be this person, on this day, in these times, experiencing these disabilities. We also assume that each person truly wishes to be heard and understood, and it is our responsibility to genuinely express our interest and commitment in a way that someone of today's younger generation can understand. Finally, we assume that we will be honest and forthright with our views, whether the person likes it or not, but we will always share this honesty with the intent of helping the person move forward, not to put anyone down, or make anyone feel small.

Temple Grandin is a renowned professor of animal science who speaks around the world on animal behavior and the humane care of animals. Her work has dramatically improved the treatment of animals in the livestock industry. Grandin is on the autism spectrum and has made a significant contribution to awareness and understanding of autism: "We all may be different within ourselves, but not less." Simplified, her mantra is, "Different, not less."[1] I love this quote because, really, it applies to every one of us.

I had an amazing opportunity to meet Temple Grandin, thanks to a dear friend, Maren McKellin, who knew one of Temple's best friends from college. Dr. Grandin was in town to give a lecture at the local high school, and Maren arranged for a small group of colleagues to meet. The last half hour was just Temple, her friend, and myself. What an opportunity! It was an amazing experience. She spoke of how video games were a dangerous threat to young adults on the spectrum as they encourage inactivity and addiction. She also talked a lot about *Temple Grandin*, the television film based on her story. I did not know until this meeting that she had been present on the set and closely consulted with the director for accuracy. This discovery made me appreciate the film that much more.

---

1   Grandin, T. (2012) *Different...Not Less: Inspiring Stories of Achievement and Successful Employment from Adults with Autism, Asperger's, and ADHD.* Arlington, TX: Future Horizons.

I had many questions and learned much from that conversation. For one, Dr. Grandin applauded the work we are doing in Autismerica, but did not like the name itself, suggesting it drew too much attention to the term "autism" and not enough to what lies beyond the diagnosis. She also explained how important it is for young adults on the spectrum to be active and constantly working with their hands and minds. I talked to her about some of my most challenging cases, and her answer was always going back to how active the person was outside of their homes, noting that if they were inactive, that problem with daily routine would inevitably be the primary cause for their issues. Talking with Temple Grandin that evening was an experience I will never forget.

As I've indicated elsewhere on these pages, I've learned over time that I should devote my first meeting with a student to getting to know him or her, and to gaining some trust. (Remember my painful lesson with Harry, back in Chapter 1?) After I get to know the student, I then focus on the specific disability and how it impacts that individual's way of seeing the world. When mutual trust is established, this process becomes much easier. I've already mentioned that parents can be a barrier, as well as a wealth of information. I assess the situation as best

I can and, if necessary, I focus my energies on both parent and student. While the classical training style tells us to look solely at the student, I've learned that without parental buy-in, it can be difficult to get the student to open up.

At this point I'd hope to have a relationship of trust with the student, and at least enough buy-in from the parents that they're comfortable with you working with their child. Then what direction do you take? In this phase of working with a student I tend to take a more behavioral approach to academic issues. You see, while a person-centered approach is very effective in establishing a baseline relationship, it is not enough by itself to help a student on the spectrum move forward. If you do not eventually shape sessions with specific goals and directions, it is possible, particularly with a spectrum student, that they will wind up in the type of academic or personal distress that requires immediate attention. Thus, when you are at a point where you can discuss issues, look at the specific things posing a problem, and try to draw as black-and-white a solution to that problem as possible.

Let's say you have Johnny, and Johnny is a very bright young man, with an exceptional memory that he has been able to rely on for most of his high school years without having to do homework. But now he's in college, and he needs to up his game. The primary reason Johnny does not do homework is his video gaming and internet habit. These behaviors keep Johnny up all night and cause him to lose track of time, resulting in poorly completed assignments.

In working with Johnny, I would work to construct a very basic realization: behavior = impact. I would write out lists that say, "If I play games more than two hours per night, I will not finish all my homework." Then, "If I do not finish my homework, I will potentially fail the course." And then, "If I fail the course, I will suffer XX consequence." In reaching XX consequence, I would consult with the parent. This is an extremely behavioral approach, but it's highly effective. I often find that spectrum students lack the ability to see beyond the immediate consequences of their behaviors, which is why lying and procrastination can be so common. The student thinks, "If I lie about my homework being finished, my parents won't get mad."

They don't go a step further to think about what will happen weeks later when the term is over; rather, they look at that one, immediate situation and do what's necessary to avoid a negative consequence in the moment.

By spelling out the consequence in black and white, and making sure all parties know what it is, students can better shape their behavior. In my session, while there is often this type of behavioral element in the conversation, I always return to my humanistic approach of talking about how it feels to suffer the stresses that accompany limitations, and to the activities the student enjoys during his or her free time, and then I bring the session back to key goals related to the student's plans for the future.

While this style—a balance of humanist and behavioral approaches—doesn't fit every situation, and of course there are exceptions, I do find it effective most of the time. It's important as a counselor to also always be open to feedback and criticism. I like to send an open-ended survey to my students, allowing them to share feedback anonymously, or sharing their name if they wish. I ask whether our sessions have been productive, and I ask the parents to fill it out as well. The best demonstrations of our effectiveness as counselors are the relationships we build with our clients. Do we look forward to working with them? Do we see progress? If not, are we being honest about it? This type of transparency and open feedback loop ensures an effective service.

Plato attributes the advice "know thyself" to his teacher Socrates. It's great advice for a teacher to give a student, and great advice for a therapist. It's important not only to really know yourself, but also to know what you value as a counselor to others. So often people in the field don't engage in this introspection. There's a long-standing joke that if you want to find the people in the world who are most confused about themselves, just walk into any counseling center! Laughter aside, however, honesty and openness are critical in this work—with our clients, and with ourselves.

I am a gay male. I came out at age 23, right before entering graduate school. Growing up in a Catholic, traditional family, I had come to view being gay as something to be ashamed of, something that would lead to pain and a probable AIDS infection. I was also extremely skinny, clumsy, and scatter-brained. Although I've never been formally diagnosed, I would probably fit the clinical criteria for attention deficit hyperactivity disorder (ADHD). Needless to say, my younger years were not very positive ones for me in terms of coming out and understanding myself on a deeper level, as a unique person with the potential to make contributions in the world.

I can remember the night I came out to my best friend. I had just been accepted into graduate school, and I thought to myself, "If I can't be honest about myself to other people, or to myself, how can I possibly help anyone else?" So I did it. I am grateful that people accepted me fully, including my family, and I was able to grow proud of who I am and embrace it. This achievement of accepting something that makes us socially unique and embracing it, regardless of disability, age, race, appearance, or anything else, is essential to self-development and actualization. It is actually rooted in a belief system written by Harlan Hahn.

Operating from a sociological perspective, Hahn's model[2] posits that any disability is merely a trait of human difference, and the experience of having a disability is more a social reaction to this human difference than the difference itself. Thus, the experience of having a disability is akin to being a member of a minority or social group in the US.

Hahn's original 1985 publication of his model is fundamentally a response to the most common model for working with disabilities at the time: the medical model of disability. In essence, this model views disability as a sickness that requires treatment with symptoms to be either cured or abated.[3]

There are many problems with this model. First, it suggests that a disability is a human flaw that requires professional treatment. Second, it assumes that a person with a disability would prefer to

---

2   Hahn, H. (1985) 'Disability policy and the problem of discrimination.' *American Behavioral Scientist 11*, 1 (January), 293–318.

3   Gill, C. J. (1999) 'Invisible ubiquity: The suprising relevance of disability issues in evaluation.' *American Journal of Evaluation 20*, 2 (Spring/Summer), 279–287.

live without it and should thus seek a cure. If given the choice, many people with disabilities would not wish for a so-called cure, as they view their disability as an essential part of themselves.[4]

Hahn's model offers an insight into the disability experience from a difference perspective. It also makes distinctions regarding the effect of a disability, particularly the social impact of one that is visible. This point seems obvious, but at the time Hahn was developing his ideas, no theory had yet detailed that people generally demonstrate an initial reaction to someone whose disability can be easily seen, perhaps by way of a wheelchair or assistance animal. The model does not omit people with "invisible" disabilities, however; on the contrary, it notes that disabilities that cannot be seen will nonetheless spur a reaction once the diagnosis becomes evident. Hahn goes even further, suggesting that reactions to disabilities on the part of others might be a product of their own internal fears.

Often when people learn that someone they know has a disability, particularly a highly visible one, they fear for their own wellbeing. They begin to experience anxiety about the possibility of developing a disability, to consider the idea that they, too, might one day be in a similar circumstance. Feelings of apprehension, acts of avoidance, and paternalistic behaviors can all ensue.[5]

Hahn's model helps explain the learning process from a relational model. Given that ultimately learning does stem from a relationship between student and teacher, this model is helpful in understanding the human dynamics surrounding disability. Over time, additional features were added to Hahn's model. Carol Gill added that not only is disability merely a trait of human difference, but it is also a cultural phenomenon that incorporates the point of view that often accompanies having a disability, including cultural values such as tolerance for others and their differences, a high tolerance for the absence of resolution, and highly developed skills in managing multiple

---

4　Edwards, R. A. R. (2005) 'Sound and fury; Or, much ado about nothing? Cochlear implants in the historical perspective.' *Journal of American History 92*, 3 (December), 892–920.

5　Hahn, H. (1985) 'Disability policy and the problem of discrimination.' *American Behavioral Scientist 11*, 1 (January), 293–318.

problems, among other attributes. Thus, in taking this thinking a step further, we can conclude that disability truly is socially constructed—it is a product of the individual and reactions to the individual in an environment.

Hahn's model is helpful because it mirrors the essence of teaching—a relationship between an instructor and a student. This emphasis on the relationship is particularly important with adult learners at community colleges. As the teacher reacts to a student with a disability who is disclosing personal accommodation needs, a reaction occurs and a change takes place. Whatever this change, it is a social product that results from an interaction between two people.

In the simplest of terms, Hahn's model says that if we view those things that make us unique as simply a part of our personality and our set of characteristics and nothing more, we grow pride and strength from those traits, allowing us to view ourselves in a much more positive light. This view is the one we, as counselors, should strive for in order to see all the dimensions of ourselves, including what we might perceive to be our flaws and limitations, and look at them as things that make us better for who we are and what we do.

For example, I can relate to students who struggle with invisible disabilities such as mental illness or learning disabilities because I have aspects of my sexuality that, when revealed, sometimes spark a positive or negative reaction. This is not to say that I understand exactly what my clients are feeling, but it does mean that I can relate to their emotions, and as a result, better empathize with them. The more honest we are as counselors with ourselves, the more we can help our clients move forward.

In conclusion, there is no formula, no one-size-fits-all for counselors. We each have our quirks, we each make mistakes, and we each grow from them. If you are a new counselor in this field, be patient with yourself. See how well you are working with others and make refinements along the way. Parents or students should also remember that we all make mistakes, and if the intentions are good, the outcome ultimately will be as well. It all boils down to our humanity and kindness in taking care of one another—we are all in this together—and we are all different, but equal.

Chapter 10

Autismerica

One of the Proudest Accomplishments of My Career

Back in 2010 I met with a parent who had a son starting at my college in the upcoming fall. She explained that her son went to a small high school where they knew of only one other student on the autism spectrum, and he was two grade levels behind her son. She said her son spent most of his time at home playing video games, but he'd like to have friends to do things with. So far, however, he just hadn't had much luck making friends at school. The mother wanted to know if there were any other new students in the college who had a similar profile, and if so, could I introduce them to one another?

Her question got me thinking: certainly, I did know other students who were in a similar or identical situation, but I wasn't really sure how to approach the process of bringing them together. I also worried that if I reached out to specific students, others might feel slighted. And what if I was just wrong in my efforts at friend matchmaking? The whole situation left me feeling puzzled, but it also struck home the idea that there must be a solution to the problem of students on the spectrum being isolated from each other.

I asked a colleague what she thought. She agreed, there were more and more students on the autism spectrum coming to college, seeking out some kind of connection, yet unsure how to forge it. We wanted to get some more specific numbers so we looked at our case files to see how many students had self-identified as either on the autism spectrum or diagnosed with Asperger's to get a sense of what we were dealing with. Combined, we knew of roughly a hundred students who were coming to the college or who were already enrolled in the college who were on the spectrum. That got us thinking: what if there was a way to get even some members of this group together? What would be the outcome?

We decided we should try to find out. Taking the risk, we sent a letter to each of the families we knew about. We picked an evening near the end of the term and encouraged students to come meet one another. We told them we had no predetermined plans on what to do once we all arrived, but hoped as a group we could find a solution to this question of how to best use our meetings together. Our only goal was to connect students with other students, and from there we would see what happened.

As soon as the letter went out, I felt nauseous. All kinds of fears came to mind: what if the weather was poor that night (the meeting was in late November)? What if nobody got along? What if there was a fire alarm? And worst of all, what if only one person came, how isolating would that be? The days leading up to the meeting felt endless, and the weather forecast wasn't looking great.

At last the night arrived. My colleague and I reserved the campus games room, with its pool and ping-pong tables. We thought the room might provide a nice recreational tone before the meeting. As the minutes came closer, my stomach was in knots: how many people would arrive? I was having flashbacks to my high school graduation party, which I unwisely scheduled the night before graduation when everyone had a million other parties to attend, leading to a low turnout. I was back in high school all over again.

The first person and his parents arrived. And then another. And another. And another. Before we knew it, we were able to count a good 40 students who were in the room, and with them, almost every one had also brought at least one parent along for support. We could tell there was a lot of resistance from the students themselves—the majority *did not* want to be there, but their parents most certainly did want them to be there, and the parents wanted to be there too.

I gathered everyone together, but I tried to separate the students as far from the parents as possible. They could only be a few rows apart, but I knew that if this was to work, the meeting had to be in a format dictated by the students. I asked them hypothetically if they got together once a month for an evening what they would enjoy doing. "Not talking," one shouted out. Another said the same thing. "Everyone always wants to talk about feelings and stuff. This stuff sucks. It's no fun." Such was the theme from the larger group in the room.

"So what do you like to do for fun?" I asked. The answer was things I already knew, but wanted to be sure: video games, watching anime, drawing, board games, and computing were the most frequent responses. Again, they reiterated: *no talking*. This message came out loud and clear. I wrote all the things down people asked for on the chalkboard.

I then turned to the parents to ask if I had missed anything. It was then that I noticed something else—most of the parents were quietly talking with one another while I was talking with their children. They were networking: talking about teachers they liked, places they were able to find their children a part-time job, and doctors who were sensitive to the unique demands of treating a child on the spectrum. I realized in that moment that the parents needed this type of meeting just as much as the students did, if not more so.

Given all this information, I made a proposal that in retrospect, I should have thought about before sharing. I asked the students, if next month I was able to get some video game systems, rent some anime movies, bring more computers, would they be willing to come again and give this another shot? While most were initially hesitant to say yes, after looking behind their backs to their parents, most acquiesced and agreed to try again. Soon after I drew the meeting to a close. I didn't have the things that were needed in that moment to make things happen, and I didn't want to set a tone for failure. We all agreed to come together again next month in December, and to try to have a good time.

After the meeting, I sent an email out to everyone who worked at my college. Luckily, I work at a pretty big school, so there were many recipients. I asked them if they had any old video game systems, board games, animated DVDs, or related things collecting dust, and might they consider donating them to my office. I contacted our library's office and arranged for several TVs and DVD players to be made available. I also moved the location to another lounge that had a few computers in the area—probably not enough for everyone, but enough to show I had made an effort to meet my end of the bargain.

Within a few days, the donations from staff members came pouring in. I was surprised how many video game systems we got, especially since most cost anywhere from $100 to $300 for even a used unit in the store. We also got lots of board games, and one unexpected donation: a tape-deck karaoke machine. The player was so old the only songs were corny ones, but still, perhaps someone might find it fun. I brought all the donations and set up all the technology a few hours before our second meeting, and again, waited nervously...

Again, there was a decent turnout, similar to the last meeting. Luckily even in December the weather had been forgiving that day. My dean had told me we could proceed with the meeting as primarily a social one using resources, as long as there was *some* kind of educational component to it. So, for the first ten minutes, I talked a little about how to do well in college if the next semester was your first one. Short, but sweet.

I then told everyone to go out and enjoy themselves. I shared what video game systems we had, what board games and videos, and crossed my fingers. Right away two-thirds of the attendees ran for the video game units. While most of the video games were on the older side, I found the type of video game didn't matter much to the students. In fact, many enjoyed the older games, taking a trip down memory lane.

My colleague and I split up and worked the room. One of us would monitor the students, making sure nobody was left out and everyone with paired with someone, unless the person specifically asked to be left alone. The other person worked with the parents, trying to connect groups together of similar level children, and encouraging conversation among the parental groups. This was a much easier job in retrospect; we learned parents are good at quickly networking and sharing information with one another to benefit their children.

Something interesting happened with most of the students who were gaming. They were interacting and socializing. It was primarily about the game they were playing, but every once in a while an effective comment would work its way into the conversation. For example, their game character would get killed, and then a student would say it reminded him of how his math teacher made him feel when docking him points for turning in his homework late. Or they would complete a level, and one would say it was as awesome as the chicken nuggets at the cafeteria. It was interesting how content worked its way into the interactions.

Similar things happened at the anime monitors and board games. The majority of a conversation would be focused on the game at hand, but content would also work its way in. Surprisingly, the karaoke machine was also a big hit. Granted, only certain students enjoyed it, and there appeared to be a preference for women to choose karaoke for whatever reason, but there were some students who utterly loved the machine, even though it was so old that sometimes the audiocassettes got caught and had to be rewound by hand.

The time flew. In fact, without my noticing it, over an hour-and-a-half passed, and we realized the building would be closing soon. I asked the group if they would like to meet again in January. This time, the answer was a resounding yes. We also thought we should come up with a name. The name, Autismerica, came from the students. This choice also surprised me, as I was throwing out names that didn't include the word "autism" or "disability." I had been taught in school that most people with disabilities like to avoid such labels. But the students actually liked that the word was in the name. Another student agreed to create a logo for the next meeting. Here it is:

In time, our numbers grew, and we are still going strong. We normally have close to 70 or 80 people in attendance at our meetings. We also started sending out invitations to the local high schools and universities in the area, inviting them to participate in our meetings. The group has become a wonderful way for students who plan to attend our school in the fall to develop a comfort level with the college before they formally begin their first year.

In addition, we added officer positions as a way to help encourage students to model appropriate social behavior. We host specialized training for interested volunteers, catered with free pizza. (I swear you can get a college student to climb a mountain if you promise a free pizza at the top of it.) We helped our student volunteers learn how to greet new members and make them feel welcome. The student officers then become far better models of appropriate behavior than we could ever be—and the other students aspire to become like them.

We wrote a grant application to Autism Speaks to procure some funding to update our video game systems and develop a mentoring program. We were able to get a $5000 grant with just a few days of proposal writing, and now our students can enjoy the newest games they love the most. For the mentoring program, which we're calling Autismerica Mentoring Program (AMP), we recently started pairing new students with current students, with great success. Students coming to the college feel all that more comfortable knowing someone is in their corner to root for them and be their mentor and friend. Mentors also benefited from a feeling of pride and a desire to be an even better student to their mentees.

In the five years since we started Autismerica, our group has met religiously, nearly every second Thursday of every month. The pattern of attendance is often the same—parents will drag their children to their first or second meeting, and then by the third or fourth it's the students who lead the way for the parents. Some parents come regularly to network with others, and some feel comfortable enough with our group that they stay at home and enjoy a night of having their home to themselves, another reward most certainly earned!

The Autismerica program is one I believe can be replicated at almost any educational institution in the world. It costs little to no money to start, other than an investment of time. We have made our group open to other schools that want to develop a chapter, and some schools have reached out to us, which makes me very proud. Should you be interested in establishing a chapter at your school and need some assistance, please feel free to visit our website at www.cod.edu/autismerica. You can contact me through a link on that page. The group has become one of the proudest experiences of my career, and I suspect that almost everyone involved with it would say something similar. I feel very lucky to have been part of this experience, and hope Autismerica lives on for many years to come.

Chapter 11

Lessons Learned from the Field of Rehabilitation Counseling for Professionals and Parents Alike

I feel very blessed to have found my occupation. In writing this book, I hope to reach colleagues who seek to broaden their knowledge or become better educators and/or therapists. To make a disclaimer: I make no argument that I consider myself to be any better or any worse at my job than any other practitioner out there, but I most certainly love the work that I do and have a passion for becoming the best I can in helping others. If you are a therapist with a similar philosophy, perhaps you will be able to draw something useful from these pages. So in this chapter I will take some time and write about my personal counseling style and share some practices I've developed over the years.

To start, my training is in an academic discipline called "rehabilitation counseling." When people hear the word "rehabilitation," they most commonly think of drug and alcohol rehabilitation or substance abuse counseling more generally. While these areas are indeed under the educational umbrella of rehabilitation counseling, there are additional sub-disciplines in the category as well. The field also addresses rehabilitation in the philosophical sense, positing that people with disabilities, and all people regardless of diagnosis, are always in a state of flux and growth—all of us building who we are as individuals and walking our own paths. For some with disabilities, this is a rehabilitative route as a result of recovery from an accident or trauma. For others, it is more about building the people we are as human beings with a diagnosis that may be congenital or permanent, but in an effort to maximize our life experiences. To quote from the Commission on the Certification on Rehabilitation Counseling (CRCC):

> Rehabilitation counselors assist individuals with physical, mental, developmental, cognitive, and emotional disabilities to achieve their personal, career and independent living goals in the most integrated setting possible. They engage in a counseling process that includes communication, goal setting, and beneficial growth or change through self-advocacy, psychological, vocational, social and behavioral interventions. Rehabilitation counselors utilize many different techniques and modalities, including assessment, diagnosis and treatment planning, counseling, case management, and advocacy to modify environmental and attitudinal barriers, placement-related services, and utilization of rehabilitation technology.[1]

While there are a very small number of bachelor's degree programs in rehabilitation designed to help prepare future master's level students, you must ultimately seek out a minimum of a master's degree. For licensure as a certified rehabilitation counselor, you must have at least a master's degree and roughly over 1600 hours of supervised rehabilitation counseling. There is also a doctorate of rehabilitation degree offered at my alma mater, Southern Illinois University at Carbondale, which also houses the Rehabilitation Institute, one of the US' largest educational facilities dedicated to the research of disabilities and personal growth. To pursue a master's degree in rehabilitation, you must typically earn a bachelor's degree in one of the social sciences such as psychology, sociology, or anthropology, or possibly in the related fields of either special education or social work. There are not a lot of master's degree programs in rehabilitation counseling in the nation—roughly about 50, usually one or two

---

1   Go to www.crccertification.com and choose "Locate a Professional."

per state. For a full list of programs in the country, see the Council on Rehabilitation (CORE) website.[2]

Training in rehabilitation counseling at master's level usually begins with a year of academic courses in subjects like vocational placement; medical and psychosocial issues of disability; counseling theories investigation; and a practical personal counseling course that enables the student to begin to develop listening and therapeutic skills. These classes are usually offered intensively, over the duration of a year in three concurrent semesters. In the second year of study, the student begins practicum and internship work (usually unpaid) at some site that serves people with disabilities and facilitates the development of practical counseling skills. This is by far the most important part of the rehabilitation counseling training. It's one thing to study different counseling styles and philosophies in a textbook; it's a far different thing to do the work in an actual setting, with real clients!

Most commonly people who obtain a degree in rehabilitation counseling work for different state agencies, mainly through the Department of Rehabilitation, a federally and state-funded program in each state that helps provide employment opportunities to people with disabilities (see Chapter 3 for more on their services). Other opportunities for employment can include educational institutions from kindergarten level all the way to college, private agencies that serve people with disabilities, and even a private practice (seeing clients one-on-one for regular therapeutic sessions).

To work in any of these positions, however, you will first need to be certified by the Commission on Rehabilitation Counselor Certification, a national agency that ensures rehabilitation counselors have the proper training and credentials to work with people with disabilities. In most cases, you must complete a minimum of 600 hours of internship experience, be supervised by an appropriate professional, and then pass an examination. You must also earn a master's degree in rehabilitation counseling. This is a long road, but most certainly attainable by a dedicated professional.

---

2   See www.cacrep.org

My internship took place at a state psychiatric center for people with severe to profoundly intellectually disabled as their primary diagnosis. By severe to profound, I'm referring mostly to people who function at an intellectual level of five years old or younger, some without any verbal skills at all. It was a residential program where most of the people would probably live for the rest of their lives. Honestly, it was in many ways a depressing place. While the staff were all very dedicated toward helping others and making a difference, there were many people who were in the later chapters of their lives, with little to no familial involvement. Many of the residents had not had a visitor for years, a reality that hit me hard.

That first job taught me the importance of planning for the future of someone with a disability. It was heartbreaking to learn that a large number of the residents had lived with one or two parents, and when those caregivers had died, they had left behind few to no arrangements to secure the future of their child. While it is a difficult reality for parents to face, it is not one to be ignored: parents probably won't outlive their children, and cannot assume the person or facility that takes over their care will give the level of love and devotion they, as parents, provided. It is extremely important to plan for this possibility in the future and to prepare children for it as well.

I remember when I first got notification that I would be doing my internship at a home where most of the clients would be lower functioning. To be honest, I was very disappointed at first. While I was excited about the prospect of being out in the field working with other people, I worried how my clinical counseling skills would develop among clients who were nonverbal, or only able to communicate intellectually at a childlike level. I thought the experience would put me at a disadvantage for my future, where I hoped to work with all kinds of people with disabilities. I feared my future skills would not fully develop as a result. I could not have been more wrong.

I learned right away that the art of counseling does have a verbal component, requiring all kinds of complex words and imagery, but more importantly, working with others involves a human component in which the level of intellect behind a person's words is irrelevant, and understanding the human spirit residing within each of us is far more important. We all feel sadness, loneliness, and pain, as well as happiness, joy, and love. This truth exists regardless of intellectual level, degree of disability, or anything else. Through my internship I learned to develop methods for understanding a person's feelings, even if that person didn't have the words to articulate them.

Now certainly I made my share of mistakes along the way. I will never forget the day I worked with a client named Angie who was nonverbal and very upset. She was stomping up and down and rocking back and forth. I went into the room, arrogantly thinking, "I'm the trained professional with all kinds of hours of training under my belt, so I can solve the issue and help Angie feel better." I pointed to objects in the room—her teddy bear, her blanket—and I tried things like changing the television channels and asking if she was hungry or needed to go to the bathroom. Nothing I tried seemed to stop her emotions. I then concluded that perhaps the situation was nothing that could be solved—perhaps she was just making noise as a means to stimulate herself, and there was no action I could take that would help. This was an easy conclusion to make, given that everything I tried failed.

Embarrassingly, this was the easy way out. I think we, as professionals, can make this error at times. We write people off and make all kinds of justifications in our mind as to why nothing is working. And we are capable of rationalizing at almost any level possible. We might think, "The energy I'm using to solve this problem could go to another person, so I owe it to that other person to move this person along to someone else so I can then focus on the next person I see." Because I didn't think I could help Angie. But although I told myself that I was applying my professional discretion, really, I was abandoning my client.

Luckily, a service technician soon entered the room and asked what was going on. She pulled Angie's file and spoke with the other nurses. She found out that Angie was crying because it was time for her medications and the nurse who administered it would always come in playing a game of "Itsy, Bitsy Spider" as Angie took the medications.

This ritual was something Angie always enjoyed. That day the nurse who normally administered her medications was sick, and so the routine was thrown off. I learned a very important lesson that day about people and how the littlest things we do can have a large ripple effect in the lives of others. Those two minutes of "Itsy, Bitsy Spider" were Angie's favorite part of the day, the most important part of the day for her, and I dismissed the problem because I couldn't determine a solution.

This experience greatly shaped my future actions. No matter what the level of functioning of a client, I would look for signs that might indicate what a person was feeling, and if I was stuck, I would find others who could interpret the client's behavior for me. I learned that nonverbal actions can also be effective ways to communicate, and that we communicate volumes with our body language, in some instances, more effectively than we ever do with our words.

I was lucky enough to have an assistantship at the university I attended. An assistantship is when you work for a college or university, and in turn the school pays your tuition. I worked at the university's disability services office—one of the greatest experiences of my professional life.

A disability services office in higher education primarily provides access to students with disabilities through the delivery of academic accommodations while following the laws and guidelines set out from a variety of federal laws including the Americans with Disabilities Act, Section 504 of the 1973 Rehabilitation Act, the 1996 Telecommunications Act, and others. By law, every university or college that receives state and/or federal funding (which is almost every school across the country) is required to have such an office.

The wonderful thing about working in disability services in higher education is the synthesis of left- and right-brain activities that it requires. There are all the legal requirements and college rules and regulations that must be followed, and conversely there are all the emotional and interpersonal demands that accompany working with students with disabilities. It really is a wonderful, stimulating combination, and I love that every day I need to draw on both creative and administrative skills to address different situations. One day you might need to explore ways to make an art appreciation class accessible to a person with visual impairments, and the next day need to work with an internship site for a student who is dyslexic and wanting to become an elementary school teacher. The potential combinations of access challenges are almost endless, and every day is unique.

After graduate school I was hooked, and I have worked in higher education ever since. My first job out of university was directing a disability services office at a community college, where I first developed my passion for community colleges. To me, they are among the most important institutions in the US. Their mission is to meet members of the community and provide education and training for their futures, regardless of their age, educational experience, or level of ability. The community college mission is genuinely noble; I thank my lucky stars almost every day that I get to participate in it.

I worked in the disability services office providing access services for almost six years, and then had the opportunity to work for the counseling center at another community college, providing therapeutic personal counseling specifically to persons with disabilities. I applied for this new position, was fortunate enough to be hired, and have been in the role for nearly 14 years. The work is particularly exciting and gratifying for me, because I serve students without the administrative burdens that can come with working in a disability services office. I am very grateful to have my wonderful job today, and hope to be doing it for a very long time.

Over the course of the past 14 years, I have had the chance to further hone my skills as a rehabilitation counselor, working almost exclusively, and directly, with students. I was also able to earn my PhD, focusing my dissertation on effective teaching interventions for students with disabilities at community college level. Chapter 12 explores some of those findings, particularly those aspects of my research that are most applicable to higher education.

Chapter 12

Effective Teaching Interventions

On most Saturdays, for three years, I attended a doctoral program in community college leadership. The program was a great chance for me to learn even more about community colleges and how they function, and more importantly to write a dissertation on a specific topic of my choosing. When studying for a doctorate, probably the largest and most important undertaking is the writing of a dissertation—a lengthy text, usually at least a hundred pages, that explores a specific research question as deeply and thoroughly as possible.

I was very lucky; my advisors gave me the freedom to write about almost any topic I chose, as long as it related to my day-to-day work and was linked to community colleges. My classmates wrote on all kinds of fascinating topics: how to improve veterans' services at community colleges for students returning from service; the critical nature of continuous improvement and accreditation to the health and future of any community college; the traits and qualities of the most effective community college presidents, and the ways they inspire others—all the research questions were interesting, and it was a delight to hear about my classmates' findings as we went through the process together. But the question loomed over my head: what do I want to research?

I knew my career would be devoted to working with students with disabilities at community college level. I knew the numbers of students on the autism spectrum were rising with every semester, and more and more creative teaching interventions would be required to address this increase. I also knew there were numerous smart, talented faculty all over the country who were doing creative things to make their classrooms more accessible. Given this surge in activity relating to my field, the answer seemed obvious: I wanted to talk to those accomplished faculty, people deemed by multiple reliable sources as being effective, and identify and learn about their best practices.

I formulated my primary research questions:

1. What do community college faculty perceive as the challenges of teaching students with disabilities?

2. What strategies have community college faculty found to be effective in assisting students with disabilities in becoming successful?

3. What actions have community college administrators taken that effectively address the issues related to success for students with disabilities?

4. How can community college administrators enhance their support of faculty who teach students with disabilities?

For the purposes of this book, I focus primarily on the findings of my first two questions, but also touch on the other two.

I created a variety of instruments to help me find highly effective college-level instructors of students with disabilities from a variety of disciplines, including speech, science, math, English, computer science, and education. I asked them myriad questions about the greatest challenges they were facing in the classroom in instructing adults with disabilities, and about the interventions they had developed to achieve success. I learned a lot in this process.

Their responses reflected four general clusters of frustrations: a need for additional college funding and staffing; a lack of knowledge of all the intricacies of all the different disability groups; challenges related to taking the appropriate steps to intervene in situations involving mental health and academic performance issues; and finally, balancing their teaching with listening to various issues some of their students bring to college, such as a lack of secondary level educational planning and maturity discrepancies.

Faculty shared many helpful examples of these challenges. For instance, at many colleges across the country a large percentage of the faculty are adjunct, or part-time, earning perhaps only a few thousand dollars for each course they instruct. They are also forced to travel to several different universities to teach their appropriate discipline and make a living. This schedule leaves little time for addressing additional issues that might arise from a disabling condition or a personal crisis. One administrator summed it up:

> It can be hard getting part-time faculty to care. We are experiencing bad economic times at the moment. Some of these folks, they're teaching seven, eight, nine courses to make a living. If you do the math, someone teaching ten courses a semester at our rate of pay, which is higher than at most community colleges, would make about $25,000. Double it and it's $50,000, and if it's the second income in the family, they can make a living in the area. So, a lot of our part-timers have a lot on their minds, and student issues sometimes throw them out of the cycle that they're counting on to survive.

Another challenge they shared was the pressure to maintain standards and balance the needs of each student. One instructor admitted there had been times she had been forgiving and perhaps gone easy on a student's grade out of sympathy and a lack of time. She did it with the best of intentions, but acknowledged that there could be poor ramifications for the student down the academic road. She shared:

> It's like I'm saying to the student, 'Now I'm going to give you a score that's not going to help you in any way but will boost your self-esteem.' It creates a domino effect. I have a different perception of the student now that I know about his disability, and I want to help out, so I will be lenient with the score. On the one hand, I have a student who's smart and who's doing his work, and he gets a B because I have this standard of what I do, but then on the other hand, I'm looking at the student with the disability, and I think, well, I'm giving you a B, but realistically your B is like a D. And then

I hope neither the other students nor the student with the disability finds out about my grading discrepancy. It hurts the integrity of the overall degree. Then I think it's my fault for building up the self-esteem of the student with disabilities instead of grading their work. We're doing a disservice to them in the college.

These were disappointing findings, but they reflect the realities of today's modern education. On a more positive note, I wanted to focus my research on the interventions that they took that were the most effective—the ways they met all these challenges head on. This proved to be much more fruitful and inspiring. Again, the issues clustered into broad categories, three this time: behavioral interventions; building relationships with students; and applying creative teaching strategies.

Some examples included being adaptable with course delivery and content, being readily available and open to receiving feedback, applying personal experiences related to disabilities to their teaching, starting relationship building at the very first meeting, allowing students to feel comfortable with self-disclosure, treating students humanely, breaking concepts down, creating instructional materials in alternative formats, using student journaling, speaking with former students for input, using positive visualization exercises to encourage success, using grading rubrics ahead of time to clearly lay out grading expectations, and delivering content through alternative and multimodal methods.

A couple of my favorite examples of these included the following:

The one thing that you have to start with is rapport. If the student doesn't feel trust, if they don't feel a rapport, you're not going to get anywhere. In the college setting, as an introductory first day activity, we'd go over the syllabus and what we will be studying in the class. I tell them upfront that I'm not going to call on them and I promise not to embarrass them in front of their peers. And I tell them not to worry if they make a mistake; we're all here to work on this together. I break the ice right at the very beginning, so from day one, I have students talking to me. They're not afraid to say something.

And another:

> Treat them like they're human beings. They may not be able to control the drooling, but they are a human being. Give them the dignity. Having a sense of humor, not making fun of them, but instead not taking everything so seriously that you can just kind of say, oh look at that, that happened, oh well. I see this sometimes with the parents' involvement. It's the kid you need to be talking to, be they a young adult or an older adult. I think it's difficult because there is discomfort, and it's people who have a sense of humor who seem to get over that discomfort. They get self-conscious. Getting over those kinds of things is important. So, people who have a sense of humor, people who really realize they are human beings, and don't see them with a 'big D' disability, that helps. That takes maturity and life experience, I think.

Nearly every instructor I interviewed in my research emphasized the importance of working with the student to determine solutions and seeking input when necessary. I liked the comment "always treat students humanely." This statement summarized things nicely. Many faculty also mentioned the importance of maintaining academic standards whenever possible, which made them effective in my eyes. There are indeed times when a student or parent makes requests that are unreasonable, and the faculty member must have the courage to say "no" to maintain the integrity of the institution and course topic. This courage is what made them inspiring—they were not afraid to say no to things, but would then move on by exploring alternatives.

When I interviewed administrators, similar themes emerged: shrinking federal and state dollars to provide services and instruction; increasing complexities in student needs and expectations; and a driving passion to find solutions to allow students to achieve their dreams. These observations again underscored the wonderful mission that community colleges have in our country.

All this research taught me the importance of the faculty–student relationship, and the value of matching students with the best possible fit in a teacher. I will try in almost every faculty in-service to meet with new instructors to get a sense of their teaching styles and experiences, and then when helping students choose classes, look for appropriate fits. It's interesting to note I found no correlation between a faculty member's experience in working with specific disability groups and their effectiveness. A good instructor can be effective with no experience working with different disability groups, as long as they come to the endeavor with an open mind and a passion to teach the subject they love in a way that allows the student to learn.

So when parents ask me what questions they should ask potential instructors, or more accurately, what questions *their student* should ask when meeting a new teacher, I tell them not to focus on breadth of experience with autism or other disabilities, but rather a teacher's openness to accommodation (note, not modification), and willingness to discuss what is and isn't working. Does the teacher have office hours? Are these at times that meet most student demand, or very early or late in the day for personal convenience? Ask instructors whether they use technology to keep grades up to date. Do they like to teach in a multimodal way (lecture, hands-on work, videos, etc.)? These are the questions that help determine the best faculty members for a student, and tell you how open and available they will be.

Chapter 13

Teaching Interpersonal Communications

My co-advisor for Autismerica, Sheryl Ebersold, and I thought it would be an interesting experiment to try to teach a class on interpersonal communications specifically for autism spectrum students. Luckily, at my school there was already an existing curriculum we could use, although it did require some modification specific to the population. We decided to limit enrollment to 15 students, and also made the decision to try not to classify students based on functioning level. Thus, we might have some students who were extremely verbal, and others who were very quiet or used alternate ways, such as technology, to communicate. These decisions posed a lot of challenges at the beginning, but in time, enhanced the depth of our course.

We structured the class so we would meet once a week for a two-hour period, with a 15-minute break midway through the session to allow people to have a mental pause from the work we were doing. The break proved especially helpful in the beginning, since the class was a stressful exercise for some of the students, who relied on the break to reset themselves. The course would run for 16 weeks. In terms of course outline, we used the following description:

Education 1110: Interpersonal Skills for Life and Work: Emphasizes understanding the student's style of communicating, exploring options and decreasing self-defeating behaviors. Includes awareness of communication variances among ethnic, racial, and gender groups. Through an experiential approach, students have an opportunity to develop more satisfying and effective interpersonal skills for enhancing personal and work relationships, self-esteem, and understanding of behavior differences among persons from diverse backgrounds (2 lecture hours).

Of the 15 students, about half enrolled in the course with the goal of improving their communication skills, and ultimately hoped to make friends either through the course or by meeting other people. The other half were there because their parents were forcing them to attend, and they weren't that interested in the topic. People who have taught a similar course tell me they preferred to limit these less committed students from staying on the course, but we found that most of them, in time, added to the class and eventually enjoyed being part of the group.

The first class or two we focused on getting to know the students and their hobbies. We knew if we ran the course like a group therapy model delivered in a neurotypical (nonautistic) format it would turn students off. We found out that many of these students had been placed in these types of groups before, and a format based on a nonautistic formula relied heavily on vague questions like "How are you feeling?" and "What is stressing you out?" These questions are too undefined for many students, and they would pick up what words were used as acceptable responses, parroting those rather than talking about what they were really thinking about.

So instead of asking them to use our language, we tried to learn theirs. We learned almost everyone in the room loved video games, and there were certain games that nearly all of them knew well. For some reason, Nintendo video games with the Mario and Luigi "Mario Brothers" cast of characters were of particular interest to most. If you're not familiar, let me give a brief description.

The Mario brothers are two video game characters who are Italian plumbers, who, in most games (and there are probably over a hundred of them in existence), are always on a quest to save the brave, but often kidnapped, Princess from the evil dragon Bowser. In the plot lines of most games Mario is the strong, short-tempered brother; Luigi is the calmer, more pensive brother. The Princess always turns out to be independent and able to take care of and rescue herself when given the opportunity, and Bowser is really not that bad a guy after all, just very misunderstood.

Our students' identification with this cast of characters makes perfect sense. Highly verbal students who over-contribute to classes would identify with Mario; quieter, more academic types, with Luigi. Young women often identified with the Princess, appreciating the fact that they are capable of taking care of themselves if just given the chance, and at certain points in their lives, all students could identify with being Bowser—the socially misunderstood, perceived-to-be-bad-guy-but-not-so-bad-at-all type. The four characters really make up the archetype of almost any young adult on the spectrum with regard to inner feelings. So we used the Mario characters as one way to identify feelings in ways our students could understand.

Another area of interest for many was Japanese anime. Anime are cartoons (although my students would probably be offended by the word "cartoon" for implying anime is childlike) that usually take on adult themes like sex, violence, pain, and overcoming hardship. They can be very graphic in nature and even sexual at times, though no more so than many books written in straight text. Anime provided us with a way to relate to our students because it taps into real emotions and adult situations, but often with magical or implausible plot lines. Characters often have magic powers or they are creatures capable of mystical behavior. By rooting itself in the imagination and creativity, anime provides a safe way for students to transition into the world of adulthood.

After our first two weeks of getting to know different video games, anime, and other types of characters our students found relatable, we started to focus on how they interacted with the outside world. Many expressed a frustration that their nonspectrum counterparts did not share their interests. Ironically, however, many wanted friendships with their nonspectrum peers. This was one of many paradoxes we helped students understand. In one exercise, we had students pair with me, and I would dominate the conversation talking about a topic I was personally interested in (for me, personally, it was travel and cooking), and allowed them to experience the frustration when a partner is fixated on something you don't really care about. This exchange helped many students start to develop insight into how they are sometimes perceived by others.

By the mid-point in the course, we had a good, shared understanding of how to communicate. We, as instructors, took the stance that our world was just as confusing and in need of mutual understanding as theirs, and that approach made a real impact on many of our students. For once, learning valuable information was not a matter of being forced to learn to navigate the nonspectrum world alone; it was two people from another place trying to understand their world just as much as they needed to grasp ours. This sense of mutual effort made students feel safe to start to really talk about what they were thinking and to develop connections with one another.

With this mutual trust established, we spent the second half of the course focusing on the ways that students would ultimately have to cope with the outside world—how to communicate properly in an interview, how to interact with others in a business situation, and how to express oneself when it came to dating and romantic relationships. We were surprised how few students had ever had someone speak to them about dating and sex—as though their disabilities rendered them nonemotional beings who resembled children and didn't need connections of this sort. Our students in the class had all kinds of questions about how to ask a person out or express interest without scaring the person away.

So, we did a lot of role-playing. Mock interviews, mock workplace scenarios, mock getting to know someone for the first time conversations, etc. We would put our chairs in a circle and have two people in the center role-play the situation. For those students who were especially socially nervous, we would move the role-play to the classroom next door and stream the conversation via Skype to make them more comfortable. Students would sometimes provide feedback in the form of different characters in class, and this was okay since we had that shared understanding. Others would give feedback that at times was pointed, and it offered an opportunity to also talk about how they may be perceived by others. The more we practiced, the more confidence students gained in their skills.

When we were nearly three-quarters of the way through, we asked the students if they would be open to us asking their parents for feedback, as well as willing to provide feedback themselves. Most were okay with this request. The feedback we got was overwhelmingly positive—the parents were seeing growth, and were seeing their children trying to communicate with the people around them. Of course, the situation wasn't perfect. A few students were showing much less growth than we had hoped for, which tied back to some simply not wanting to be in the class. It seemed the more adamantly the students themselves believed they didn't need the class, the less favorable feedback we received from parents, and the less favorable from their children as well. I would say, though, that 90 percent of the respondents, parents and students alike, gave the class extremely positive reviews.

Toward the end of the course we focused on closure, mostly through exercises designed to help the students take what they had learned in the course and apply it to their lives in the outside world. One interesting, rewarding dynamic that emerged was a new involvement in friendships. Many had entered the class with an interest in forming friendships with nonspectrum students, but not expressing much desire to know more people like themselves. Ironically, those very students were now hanging out together a lot and enjoying each other's company. Some strong friendships emerged in the course, and all 15 of the students, even those not interested in the course, seemed to keep an eye out for one another. A kind of family dynamic had emerged, and now these students weren't alone in navigating the complexities of college. This outcome was the most positive one of all.

Another wonderful outcome was evident in students from the course taking their personal advocacy a step further. Like Hahn's model, they wanted to share with pride that they were on the spectrum and encourage others to "come out." Two of our students became new student orientation leaders where they would greet new students to the college and give tours of the campus and answer questions.

They would speak with pride about being on the spectrum, and became active in our Autismerica group. As a result of their openness, some new students connected with them and shared that they, too, were on the spectrum. Our students had become big brothers and sisters to new students, and were idolized as role models of sorts! It was wonderfully gratifying.

We offered the course again a year later with similar results, and now experience this process with students annually. Each year we get better at screening students and developing social exercises and role-playing scenarios. We agreed to always allow any student who registered for the course to take it, even those who were forced into it by their parents. We also allow any student on any level of communication ability to participate. This approach has added additional challenges, as some students are extremely verbal, and others nonverbal, but we stand by our decision.

I'd like to emphasize that this type of program is not something that can only be offered by some credentialed therapist with all kinds of licenses and degrees. Really, almost anyone with the time and interest could be a facilitator. Although having a strong mental health background and training is of help, it is not essential. However, you do need at least two people who are very interested in the topic and willing to try to understand communication on *both* a spectrum and nonspectrum level. Speech instructors can be good at this, professionals who communicate a lot for a living, or almost any professional willing to do the research can create a similar kind of learning environment. If you work for a college with a lot of students who feel disconnected, a class like ours can be a great way to facilitate relationship building.

In conclusion, offering a class like "Education 1110: Interpersonal Skills for Life and Work" is just one of many ways you can help people connect to one another. The Autismerica model is another, and I've heard of many other models as well. Another program in our area is called the Western DuPage Special Recreation Association (WDSRA, www.wdsra.com). Although primarily targeted towards developmental disabilities, families can register their fellow members for a variety of recreational activities including camps, bowling, dances, outings, movies, and much more. It is a wonderful organization that steadfastly works to develop human connections between people.

My point is that there is no one set formula for teaching human interaction and connection. It takes creativity, patience, and innovation, but there are multiple ways of reaching the same result. Parents or adults seeking to develop a program for young adults on the spectrum can use the internet, schools, or local social workers to find others who share their interest in making a difference. I can assure you there are almost always others in a similar situation. The more creative strategies we use, the more connected we become. And should you develop something successful, please make sure to share your progress with the world (especially me!).

Chapter 14

What Students on the Spectrum Want the Rest of Us to Know

When a colleague of mine heard I was writing this book, she asked me to include a chapter that I immediately realized I wanted to write: what are the things people on the spectrum wish we knew? This is such a good question. So often, we therapists assume we know the most about this topic because of our professional vantage point. A therapist acquires confidence based on experience and a commitment to training, working hard to help others. Likewise, a parent assumes that nobody can know their child better than they do. Although both therapists and parents have these good intentions, when I started to ask students themselves about how much the people around them knew—and didn't know—about them, I was surprised how often my belief system fell short.

I asked my student Susan what she wanted nonspectrum adults to know about her. She said immediately that she is capable of much more than people think she is. This is a common initial response to the question, and it reflects inner pride, so I was pleased to hear it. Still, I told Susan I wanted a deeper understanding of her day-to-day life.

"The world is so noisy," she said. "Everyone and everything is trying to get your attention. There's always some kind of flashing something or place or thing making a lot of racket. And people expect you to make eye contact with them. I don't understand what the big deal is about this. They say that seeing in someone's eyes is like seeing in their soul or something like that, but is it really? If I have to do something that makes me uncomfortable, how is this proving anything?" I know a lot has been written and said about eye contact, but I liked the way she explained her point of view. It goes back to that question of who is to say what are appropriate social rules for interaction, and if the goal of interaction is for people to feel like themselves, why should it be required at all?

"Growing up was hard for me because it seemed like a lot of the things I cared about other people didn't. And they would get annoyed and make fun of me for it. I preferred talking to adults because they at least understood me more or pretended to understand." This comment speaks to another point I'd often heard from parents—their children tended to prefer talking to teachers rather than their classmates. And they preferred being alone much of the time as a way to avoid the stress of expectation. I asked another student, José, the same question. He said that a lot of people didn't understand how often he got stressed out and how real it felt to him. "I had a counselor in high school who asked me to rate on a one-to-ten scale how upset I was. I would always say ten to everything and he would laugh sometimes and say the situation was really more of a two or three. But he can say this because he doesn't have to live it like me. The stress really is a ten to me and even if it is a ten every time, so what!" His point reminded me that stress and the way we react to things is subjective. If we don't have the right coping skills, every situation can be a ten. It reminded me how important it was to try to find ways to help students break down stressful situations and more accurately measure their impact.

I can remember a time in my life when I struggled significantly with chronic anxiety. I was on sabbatical leave to write my dissertation, which I was grateful for, but there was also an expectation that it would be finished at the end of that four-month absence from my job. While many others in academic work handle this situation fine, I put an excessive level of stress on myself. I fixated on what would happen if I didn't finish my dissertation, how I might lose my job, the respect of my peers, and faith in myself. I also worried about the financial consequences of not acquiring my PhD. As a result, my sleep patterns greatly suffered, and my reaction to the smallest of stressors would be a "ten," as John had claimed. My ability to be objective about things disappeared as time went on, and toward the end of the sabbatical, I was a bundle of nerves, a mess, actually.

Physiologically the stress took a toll on me as well. I lost 20 pounds, my heart rate was always elevated, and sometimes I would shake for no apparent reason. I barely slept. I can recall nights where I literally stayed up all night. Looking back, I think I would label this behavior as mania. I had allowed my anxiety to get the best of me and lost all control. I sought out a therapist and psychiatrist for treatment, which started to help. It was truly the lowest point in my life; I had never known what it was like to be so distressed that I felt out of control and beyond help. And the paradox was that in part of my mind, I knew I was blowing everything out of proportion—that this state would pass, and ultimately my life would resume. But for some reason I couldn't logically tap into that part of my mind where I might find relief—it was like my anxiety was preventing me from being able to cope and heal, and I could only focus on the negative consequences.

Luckily, by the mercy of God (and a dissertation advisor with the patience of God and a partner with unlimited love for me) I finished, and somehow the anxiety levels dissipated. Therapy and medications also helped a lot. Eventually I didn't need medication or regular therapeutic treatment, but I still keep in touch and periodically meet with my therapist. We have a stigma about mental illness in our society, and people are ashamed to talk about it. Now I see my experience as one that is painful for me to recall but also as a badge of pride. These horrible experiences made me understand anxiety and depression in a much truer way than I ever would have had I not gone through this difficult time.

I related this story to another student, Gino, and he nodded his head in agreement. Gino said that day-to-day he felt hopeless and trapped. While I can never know exactly what his experience was in comparison to mine, I could relate to that feeling of knowing every day that you will consistently have negative reactions to certain stressors—changes in schedule, weather, bad reactions from work, etc. I can only imagine someone else's level of exhaustion.

The students who opened up to me shared something else they wanted people to know about them: their frustration with some expected world view. Who are we, as nonspectrum adults, to say that the way we perceive the world is the correct one? What's wrong with wanting to use technology frequently and escape to imaginary worlds as long as we return to the practical one when necessary? This is a valid question. I think the thing that is missing for a lot of college-level students, however, is knowing how to define boundaries on this type of escapism. The message they are getting from adults like me is that retreating into the worlds of technology and anime is wrong. This isn't the message we are communicating, but it is what they hear. The message we hoped they would pick up is that escaping is okay, *as long as it is in moderation*. The challenge is for us to get students to see what moderation actually is. I've learned that the more black and white we can draw this, the better it will be for students.

As I noted in Chapter 5 on technology, I encourage families to write specific formulas. For example, "You can game for two hours but must then do homework afterward." This must be black and white. I encourage parents to use a timer to monitor time, and when it goes off, to turn the game system off. Because gaming can be done online, and most college work requires a computer, I also encourage them to check their child's browser history afterwards to be sure work is being done. It sounds overly parental for a young adult, I know, but after a few weeks of this, the student is able to better internalize a sense of time and then doesn't need this degree of supervision going forward.

Back to what students on the spectrum want the rest of us to know. The final theme many students shared with me is that they do feel emotions and get lonely, like all of us. While this point seemed obvious to me, I didn't realize how many people think that fellow human beings on the spectrum do not feel emotions. "I don't talk much but I do like being around other people," one student shared. "I talk too much, I know, but I do care about others' feelings," another said. He was reminding me that it's easy to make snap judgments and negative assumptions based on what we see. One student said, "I cry a lot on the inside but you just can't see it." Among every insight students shared on this subject, this confession affected me the most. When people are quiet, we assume they choose to be that way, but that is not always the case.

We must make an effort to understand a person's world view and then make an effort for that person to understand ours. This exchange is essential to any positive relationship. I'm reminded most people do yearn for this mutual understanding, but often spectrum students lack the basic vocabulary and conceptual framework to try to achieve it. I like to believe that if I can understand someone else's world view, then perhaps I can get that person to understand mine. Depending upon the circumstances, my view might be the one necessary for success in our shared endeavor, but in other situations, perhaps it is the other way around, where the other person has the insight the situation requires.

Chapter 15

What I Wish Parents, Students, and Everyone Else Would Know

After working with families for many years, I have come to see parents as their child's greatest ally—and also their greatest foe. This view has nothing to do with any child's disability, and everything to do with *parents simply being parents*. This chapter in particular emphasizes the parent–child relationship, particularly on the things parents can do throughout their child's adolescence to help empower that child to be successful. While some colleagues of mine might parent-bash in this section, please be assured that I am not about to do so. Parents have generally been through a lot, and this book seeks to provide support, not criticism.

Anyone trying to navigate the road from childhood to adulthood on behalf of a person with a disability knows that the US education system is a particularly gnarly stretch in the journey. Life is constant IEP meetings, paperwork, and interactions with special education instructors who are deeply dedicated to their craft, but horribly overworked, underpaid, and sorely in need of resources. Frustrations can leak out into the relationship between a family and special education providers, often resulting in parents calling a school "highly adversarial" or "providing services my kid doesn't need." I always try to avoid passing judgment since I'm not hearing the other side of the story. It's critical that parents and providers alike try to see both sides. We all work to make the decisions we believe will be best for the child, and things would be so much easier for all of us if we more frequently reminded ourselves to respect the other person's point of view.

Fortunately, there are many things that parents can do, ways they can encourage their children over the long haul of growing up and graduating from high school. Obviously, they need to be as engaged as possible, attending IEP meetings, asking questions, letting the school know they are—and always will be—active participants. I realize this role can be extremely difficult, especially if one or both parents work full-time, but it is important to demonstrate full commitment. Parents should also make sure their child is an active participant in meetings. Children should be able to name their disability and, from an early age, be capable of articulating how it impacts them in educational situations. This understanding and acceptance is also needed by parents, who should do their own personal inventory of their feelings about disabilities—especially of developmental and learning ones—as any behavior that might indicate a lack of acceptance will certainly affect the child's perception of him or herself.

I remember a meeting with Abe and his father. I knew Abe had a disability, but I didn't know the details, so I asked Abe my standard first meeting questions: "What is your disability, and how does it impact you?" Abe's dad quickly interrupted, "We don't like the word 'disabilities.' Abe has some slight limitations and learns differently, but I would not go so far to say it is a disability." I then proceeded to ask Abe the question again. He couldn't even give it a name! Instead, he said, "I'm on an IEP, that's all I really know." I'm saddened by how many students have a similar response; they don't know their diagnosis. Parents may think they are protecting their child by trying to hide or minimize a disability, but this perceived form of protection couldn't be more misguided. By covering up the disability, the parent sends the child into the world with only the child's imagination to fill in the blanks, and this imagination in most cases will go to a much worse diagnosis than the real one.

If educators (including teachers, counselors, and administrators) suspect a disability—should any of them see signs of any type of disability—it is the school system's obligation to provide a diagnosis.

While the suspicion of a disability does not require its diagnosis, the system is obliged to follow the protocol until there is some determination either way. And only qualified, licensed professionals can make the diagnosis—this person can be an employee of the school or an outsider with the proper credentials. In most cases, a psychologist or learning specialist will conduct a variety of diagnostic tests to determine whether a disability is present. This initial process often involves some of the most thorough testing available, to ensure an accurate diagnosis. In fact, subsequent testing is usually less detailed, as it can be conducted by instructional assistants or teachers rather than psychologists (given the high number of students most school systems must serve). The initial diagnosis, however, is almost always very detailed in its determination in order to ensure it is accurate and proper. While the process leading to the diagnosis must be a careful one, especially given the potential impact of the diagnosis on that child's future, a thorough explanation of the diagnosis is not always passed on to the child and their parents.

Given this tendency for large school systems to be overwhelmed and to provide insufficient information to families after testing, parents should request a meeting for them and their child; they should sit down with the diagnosing professional and ask for a detailed review of the completed testing. If the testing centered on learning disabilities, they should ask for an explanation of the IQ and achievement tests conducted. Usually the tests include the Wechsler Adult Intelligence Scale and the Woodcock-Johnson Tests of Cognitive Abilities. These provide a good, detailed look at a student's learning capacities and limitations, and families shouldn't be afraid to ask questions. What do the numbers mean? What are the student's strengths and weaknesses? They shouldn't just settle for an LD (learning disabilities) diagnosis and move on. Rather, they should request an explanation, and do whatever possible to have it provided on a level that both the parent and child can understand. It's important to know what the results mean.

When a school system tests for autism, it is usually done in the form of self-reporting inventories, in which parents, the student, and educators make notes about behavioral consistencies. Again, even if the diagnosis is obvious, parents should ask for as much information as they can about where possible future deficits might arise, and what learning modalities are the strongest for their child.

Once parents have the substantive information they deserve from the school testing professionals, they need to work with their child, practicing ways for the child to articulate the disability and to self-advocate, making certain that there is plenty of inspiring information about people with similar diagnoses who have been successful. Children should be encouraged to see their disability as merely another dimension or characteristic, like eye color, hair color, height, race, gender, etc. There are many stigmas surrounding disabilities in today's society; dismantling them early on raises self-confidence and self-esteem.

When the student nears the end of high school, an assessment should be done as close to graduation day as possible, but not one day afterward, as often schools will not then pay for it. This timing is especially important if a student has learning disabilities, as some universities and accrediting boards with certification exams (nursing, investing, etc.) require that a student's documentation be no more than three years old. Once a student graduates from high school, all testing must be paid for by the family, and LD testing can be very expensive, ranging anywhere from $500 to $1500, so having recent test results serves the student's best interests.

Before high school graduation day, parents should also encourage their children to seek some type of employment, if possible. Many great qualities come from having a part-time job, even if it's only for a few hours a week. A job keeps the student busy and productive. Those hours spent on the job can curb the hours spent video gaming or online surfing. A job also teaches the student that work is a necessity for most adults. Only rarely is a disability so extreme that employment becomes impossible. I am a firm believer that we all have something to contribute to the world.

One of the things I really love about working with adults with autism is their honesty. They are usually very frank in asking questions and making observations. I have had students point out to me that I'm gaining weight (when I obviously am); tell me when it's obvious I'm not focusing fully on the task at hand; and ask me very direct questions like, "Why do I have to work as an adult?" and "Why must I study in school?" I love these questions, because they are deep ones that we should all pause and ask ourselves sometimes. Of course, there are social mores that everyone in the modern world is expected to follow, but it is healthy to question those established customs from time to time.

It is important for parents to have discussions about how their child sees the world, and what questions regularly occur to them. They should talk with their children about the necessity and benefits of work as they are growing up. Children need to understand through honest and direct communication why they cannot stay at home forever not earning any money while their parents pay the bills. They need to know that one day they will be expected to live independently and assume financial responsibility for their own futures. And they need to know that to achieve these goals, a job is essential. Remember, while these are unspoken expectations most children entering college already have in mind, spectrum students will go deeper and question these rules, and if the expectations are not discussed pragmatically, they will form their own, in their own minds. They will build logical arguments regarding why they need not apply the rules to themselves. This questioning is not out of laziness, but rather born out of a different, unique way of looking at the world—a view that does have value!

So ideally, when students arrive at my office, they have a sense of what their disability is, they've worked some kind of job so they understand what work involves, and why it is an essential element for adulthood. And ideally, given all this information, they are ready to commit to a plan of action.

Here is what I consider the worst-case scenario for a new student. First, the student does not even want to be present at the meeting. They are irritated that this obligation has taken them away from their video gaming, or they would rather be surfing the internet. The student would like to get back to a preferred activity as quickly as possible. Second, the parent does all the talking for the student at the meeting.

"John wants to get his degree and transfer to a university," the parent will say; but when I ask John, he responds, "I guess." Also, the student has had no work experience—other than perhaps a mock work experience held by the student's high school that really wasn't much of an experience at all, but rather a way to fill up the student's school days—so they have no understanding of the value and importance of work in the modern world.

In this worst-case scenario, the student often appears to be someone who has a chance of being successful in college. Grades are Cs but passing, ACT scores are on the average side, and IEPs are filled with positive comments about how likable the student is, but make little to no mention of their capacity to actually handle college work. When I see this combination of information, I see a possible red flag indicating that the student was passed on, and with heavy parental involvement in the homework, was able to pass high school courses. Parents really should not do their child's homework—*there is nothing worse they can do!*

Speaking of college, remember that it is not a required next step. As I've discussed throughout this book, there are many roads to a successful future. If a child does not want to go on with formal education and parents force it, a great deal of effort will go into proving them wrong. And the statement, "I pay the bills, so either you go to school or leave home" is not a choice. These are often realistic and pragmatic young adults—they know the parent won't kick them out of the house—and they will call a parent's bluff, either directly or indirectly. When parents have a child like this, I encourage them not to insist on college and forfeit a lot of money in tuition. I try to help them find a full-time job for their child, and see what they think of the experience. They might like it better, but more realistically they will not. The lesson will be that it can be much harder to command a living wage without some degree of advanced education. Taking a year off formal schooling to gain this realization can sometimes be just the thing and install a newfound interest in college.

I get a little upset whenever a parent says, "John/Jane is a poor test taker." In college, almost everything is tests! For many, many occupations, including my own, certification examinations to be licensed to work are entirely based on examinations. "Poor test taking" is not an excuse—and if a student is solely passing classes in high school based on homework and failing test scores, I would argue that this is not passing at all. Parents need to address the issue immediately, by understanding why exactly their child is not passing tests. Is it a matter of not being prepared? Test anxiety? Something else? They should reach out to teachers for help and even get a tutor if necessary.

After reading all of this advice, parents might feel a little on the defensive: "Well my child *does* have a disability, and so we must take this expectation into account!" Absolutely. Accommodations must be delivered appropriately to students, and instructors need to be adaptable in their teaching styles to be as multimodal as possible to reach as many students as they can. Schools must be informed of how services are going, and give updates to families. Open communication is a must.

I also acknowledge that parental involvement is a critical factor in student success. In the traditional higher education model, keeping parents out of the equation as much as possible is considered a critical element for the transition to adulthood; for students on the autism spectrum, however, these lines are blurrier. Throughout this book I have tried to share how parents are integral and can be the best advocates for their children. In fact, I've come to learn that in many cases, parental participation is essential—it is only the degree of participation that is up for discussion.

So back to the things I wish parents knew. We've covered a lot of these views already, but most importantly I wish parents knew that all children are capable of contributing to the world in their adulthood, and all are capable of many, many things. It is important, however, to seek out as much input from as many people as possible to aid the student in making realistic and attainable future goals. Should we set the bar too high or too low for children, this will lead to feelings of either inadequacy or failure regarding their futures. Let me give examples of both.

In terms of setting the bar too high, I can recall one parent of a child on the spectrum whose child, Andrew, was intellectually very low functioning. In fact, IQ testing placed the young man at the borderline range of intellectual functioning. The parent pushed the child through high school, and wanted him to use college as a pathway to a job in the medical field. To pursue almost any health occupation, college students must take a medical terminology course in the first semester, which requires a great deal of memorization and application of different medical terms. The course was overwhelming to the student, who failed every exam. Regularly completing the homework had a very small impact on the overall grade.

The parent had Andrew repeat the course three times. By the third time around, he had finally learned enough to squeak by with a D, although I suspected it was a mercy grade from an instructor hoping to avoid having the student for a fourth time. The D allowed the student to finally move forward in the coursework. Andrew was obviously unhappy, and certainly tired of taking the same class over and over, and asked me, "If I had to take the first class three times, how long will the second one take?" Still, the parent pushed forward. While I encouraged alternative career exploration, the parent was not having any of it; sure enough, the second course was exponentially more difficult than the first, and finally the family gave up and Andrew dropped out—but I'm certain he walked away with a sense of failure that could have been avoided had he not been pushed into an academic pathway that wasn't the right fit for him.

Setting the bar too low can have a similar outcome. I can think of an example of a family with a child named Maria, of average intellectual functioning, and certainly capable of attending college on a full-time basis of at least four or five classes a semester. The parents, however, wanted to go very slow on Maria's studies. "We don't want her to get overwhelmed," they said. We set out on a pattern of only one or two classes a semester for over two years. In the meantime, with all the free time the student had, she played lots of video games and engaged in online chatting, and formed a rather strong addiction—gaming for 12 or 13 hours per day. As the addiction increased, her commitment to studies decreased, and each semester Maria's grades went lower and lower. I'm reminded of my mother saying to me, "idle hands are the devil's workshop," which means (to me at least) too much free time can be dangerous. In Maria's situation, I saw that phrase come to life.

So, to review, what are the things students should bring to college to be successful, and what does every parent need to know?

★ Understanding of their diagnosis

★ Some ability to self-advocate, even if on a very basic level

★ Ability to succeed in education for classes that are homework-based or exam-based

★ Some type of outside work experience

★ A desire to continue with their education (important!)

★ Some ability to manage time to do homework successfully and independently

★ Minimal involvement of parents in completing homework (if any!)

★ An ability to control and monitor their degree of gaming and technology use

★ A parent(s) with a realistic understanding and expectation of their child's abilities, strengths, and deficits

★ A parental openness to continuing to be involved in their child's education (with limits).

Certainly, there are more things to add, but this list makes a good start. I fully and strongly acknowledge that this list is very difficult for any family to achieve, especially if the family has additional children, financial limitations that allow only minimal participation, or any other outside responsibility that can be equally overwhelming. Truly, truly, truly this can be a challenge, and parents have my full appreciation and empathy for the challenges that rise along the way. The road is not an easy one, but I'm sure they're not the first people who can attest to that!

At this point we've talked a lot about what I wish parents knew, but what about students? I am a strong believer in the concept of dyadic relationships. We learn the most when we acknowledge that both participants in a relationship are teaching and learning from each other. So, I thought it would be interesting to turn the tables and ask students to ask me what I thought they wanted me to know about them. Those who had worked with me a lot knew a lot of what I would say ahead of time, but there were also some surprises.

Incidentally, one thing that I wished future students would know is that college will be an entirely different experience from high school. I don't want to harp on about the secondary school systems because I think they are riddled with all kinds of unrealistic expectations and challenges, from having to report to parents who might be disconnected from reality, to an IEP system that is overly dependent on paperwork and too deadline-intensive, to administrators grappling with too many rules and expectations. The system, in many ways, is a mess, and I extend my profound respect and gratitude to anyone who works in this field. Indeed, I am told that the turnover rate for special education professionals is among the highest in K-12 instruction, and I understand why. I cannot begin to imagine the stresses special education teachers and counselors face.

More often than not, however, I see students fitting into one of four distinct categories. I'd like to outline each of them here, although you will recognize the characteristics and behaviors from earlier descriptions in this book. Parents might see themselves in one or all of these groupings. If they do, they should take heart: we are all human!

The first group comprises the extremely high-functioning Asperger's students who breezed through high school with little difficulty. Let's call these the "Achiever types." Achievers make it through school without having to do much homework because they either have exceptional memories or really are intellectually bright. Their ability to attend to detail sometimes even leads to them correcting their instructors! They can also often "fly under the radar" and be given breaks because, in comparison to their other spectrum counterparts, they struggle less academically, and their instructors are impressed and appreciative of them, which results in their getting a break at times. Their quirkiness is often, on a surface level, very charismatic and charming, and they can be quick to please their instructors.

Often when Achiever types get to college they really struggle because they haven't learned the discipline required for college. As I noted back in Chapter 2, in high school, homework tends to be more emphasized than examinations, so if a person has an exceptional memory or is extremely bright, passing a class isn't all that difficult.

Because Achiever types are struggling academically for the first time, they often don't seek out help because they aren't accustomed to needing it. Thus, the request for help usually comes too late. Sometimes parents also have unrealistic expectations and think their children don't need much help. I've had parents tell me, "My son is too high functioning for services." When I hear this, an alarm goes off in my head because most often the student does need services. In working with Achiever types, we, as counselors, should work to educate students and parents how to realistically gauge success and expectations, especially when it comes to homework. Time management skills truly are essential.

Those students who may have behavioral issues or intellectual issues, but who have been pushed through the system anyway, are the second type. Let's call them "Proxy students," because there is always somebody representing them, and usually in the wrong direction. Most often, Proxy students are represented by very demanding parents who insist that their child will go to college and succeed there. Often they are not being realistic about their children and their abilities. Their catchphrase is, "Maggie is capable of so much more than people see!" When we look closely at Proxy students we usually see a parent who is finishing the homework, doing all the talking in IEP meetings, and not recognizing that their child has very little investment in a plan that isn't their own.

The problem with this is that it perpetuates a parental relationship into adulthood. If the child looks at their education as an expectation rather than a desire, similar to the way they see their chores and household responsibilities, they are likely to wish to remain a part of the household, *as a child*, for the rest of their lives. There is no catalyst for moving into adulthood.

Another type of Proxy student is the one who presents behavioral issues such as being overly talkative or providing too much of a classroom distraction, so instructors push them through the system rather than slowing things down and putting the energy into that individual student while still successfully teaching their courses. And sometimes, they are right to put their teaching ahead of a single student. These students can require a lot of attention, and the sad reality is that our educational system fails in providing the resources necessary for them to be successful. This is not the fault of educators, but of the larger system, which is not providing the resources the Proxy student needs.

The best thing for a Proxy student is for the parents to come to meetings with college representatives with open minds and a willingness to take a back seat. They also need to come with the expectation that perhaps their child isn't as college-ready as they might think, and developmental or preparatory coursework is an opportunity to build a foundation for college success, not a punishment. They must consistently express pride and confidence in their children and their abilities because children often translate their parents' dominance as a lack of confidence in themselves. I am a firm believer that failure can elicit some of the greatest learning experiences in college, and I would even argue that it is a necessary part of the transition to adulthood.

Those who genuinely fall through the cracks are the third type of student. Let's call them the "Forgotten students." The Forgotten students are the ones who are genuinely putting effort into their education, their parents do trust their school systems and don't over-represent them, but for whatever reason, they were not much noticed in high school. They are often very quiet, and do decently in school, and rarely express their needs. Because of this reticence to call attention to themselves, we, adults, assume that they are fine and ready for the next step. Inside, however, they are often struggling with anxiety, or are very scatter-brained, even though we don't see it. The Forgotten students might be dually diagnosed with autism and anxiety and/or internalized ADHD, but often people have not been paying enough attention for this diagnosis to be made.

The Forgotten are those who don't say anything about how things really are going. When their parents ask, they will usually say, "College is fine." And when they meet with me, they will say, "I'm doing well in all my classes" and not much else. And in their minds, they are doing fine. They are regularly going to class, they are turning some kind of homework in, and are completing all their exams. In high school, sometimes this is all that is necessary to be successful, so they aren't ready for the changes that college brings.

But when we probe deeper, their homework, if required, has not been done well, or their grades are extremely low, test grades are abysmal, and their class participation is nonexistent. When the end of the semester arrives and they have failed their classes, almost everyone is surprised. Parents and less-experienced counselors will say, "But it seemed like she was doing well." Or, "He said everything was fine!" And usually, even in the student's mind, everything was indeed fine.

Forgotten students haven't learned how to gauge if things are going well in school or not. They also don't know how to ask for help (or don't think they need it), and will sometimes lie about their situation to avoid getting into trouble with their parents or caseworkers. It is important to help them in developing black-and-white means to calculate their grades at all times, and to make this information accessible to as many people as they are willing to allow, at least early on. This system allows someone to challenge their mistaken beliefs about how they are doing, and shows them how to actually be a success.

Those who really are ready for college, and who struggle instead with the typical issues that challenge all college students, are the final group. Let's call this group the "Ready students." Ready students do know how to do homework, how to ask for help (although it may still be difficult), and have some kind of support system that sees them for who they really are, with some degree of investment in them. There's eagerness among these students and their support network to continue with education. Although this group is the most successful, they, too, like all of us, can have their difficulties.

I find that Ready students struggle with time management and organization skills. They are very invested in being successful and graduating, but the degree of detail and time management expected for college can be overwhelming, not only for spectrum students, but also for *all* college students. Higher education is just a different ball game, and the rules are different. Instead of meeting daily from Monday through Friday, many classes only meet once or twice, maybe three times a week, and reminders about homework and due dates are not as frequent as they were in high school.

College often also requires more social skills. Almost every college requires a speech course before graduation, and often required classes will include at least one group project. These interactions can be especially stressful for any college student, but even more so for a spectrum student. Not only are there the academic expectations of the assignment, but there are also the social expectations of their peers. I have heard so many horror stories of students being alienated from group projects or having all the work dumped on them for a group project because their student counterparts just didn't know how to work with them.

So, for Ready students, we try to build in supports that help them develop organizational skills. The best outcome is to pair them with someone—ideally someone associated with the college, but if not, an outsider whom they trust—to meet with them weekly to talk about what is due and what is going on in class. Having this consistent reporting and outside opinion can really make a difference.

Back to the original premise of this chapter. The thing I most wish students knew is that any one of these types of students, as well as those who don't fit into any of these categories, is capable of collegiate success. The key is to identify the problem areas as quickly as possible, and then invest the energy necessary to address them. Because I am a counselor for all students with disabilities, I cannot tell you how many students I've seen succeed through the years. I have worked with students with significant physical, emotional, learning, and cognitive issues and seen them graduate. The severity of the disability is never the determining factor; it is the degree of investment they have in their own education. The more attention and planning, the more success. No matter who you are, success is a possibility—it may not be the success others would expect, it may not be a college degree—it might be a certificate, or it might just be life experience—but *all students are capable of self-growth and achievement.* It is just a matter of setting the right goals and breaking them down into realistic, achievable steps along the way.

Chapter 16

Taking Care of Yourself

I remember an important meeting with my own college counselor 20 years ago. I told her that I wanted to pursue a career as a rehabilitation counselor, to try to make a difference in the lives of young people and adults with disabilities. The very first thing out of my counselor's mouth was, "Make sure you avoid burnout." I didn't really understand what that meant at the time, but I do now. My first year as a counselor I often took the concerns of my clients home with me, worrying about them well into the night. I even gave a few of them my cell phone number in case they had an emergency and had nowhere to turn. Not only was this behavior crossing a professional line, it was also setting myself up for burnout. We can only make a difference in the lives of others if we take care of ourselves along the way.

Parents can have the same problem, although for them, the challenge is even greater, as they are in contact with their child every day. Watching their child's life unfold can become a 24-hour, seven-day-a-week job, with no break in sight. And for parents, taking time out for themselves can seem like a selfish and impossible thing to do. All this pressure to parent without any time off can harm all other relationships.

When we look at the research, we know that parents of autistic children often divorce. In fact, the divorce rate among these parents is nearly 80 percent.[1] The more severe the disability, the higher the risk of divorce. This statistic always saddens me because parents of children with disabilities are some of the world's most powerful and patient people. Sadly, though, the complexities of raising a child with

---

1   Naseef, R. and Freedman, B. (2012) 'A diagnosis of autism is not a prognosis of divorce.' *Autism Advocate* 62 (Fall), 1, 9–12.

unique challenges can sometimes be too much for a marriage to bear. I mention these concerns not to scare parents, but to acknowledge that in working with students I have often found that only one parent is really involved, which intensifies the pressure on the family. One of my most important jobs as a therapist is to do as much as I can to make the parent and student feel empowered to work together toward a mutual goal, and, if the parent doesn't have a partner, to acknowledge the difficulty of raising a child alone.

In the years I've been doing this work I've learned much from parents and from my fellow service providers. I've come up with the following credos, to remind both parents and professionals who work with those on the spectrum of their humanity, and to encourage them to carry on for just one more day when they're at the point of exhaustion. We have all been there, and more importantly, none of us is alone. I hope these words of advice will help.

A creed for parents of a child
on the autism spectrum

There is no greater job I can do than be the best possible parent to my child. To that effect, I will always work hard to encourage:

Love

Independence

Happiness

Safety

Security

Communication (no matter what level)

Understanding

Intellectual development

Challenge

Growth

Relationships

Skills

Values

Identity

Confidence

and Freedom.

I also recognize that to do my part in achieving these goals, I must also take care of myself. Therefore, I must turn to myself and to those I love to help me develop:

Love

Independence

Happiness

Safety

Security

Communication (no matter what level)

Understanding

Intellectual development

Challenge

Growth

Relationships

Skills

Values

Identity

Confidence

and Freedom.

I am strong, but I cannot do this job alone. It is okay to ask others for help. It is okay to take care of myself, and it is okay to express my needs to the world. Even the strongest of trees cannot shelter its own roots if it does not seek water to grow. I am human, and I am enough. My love is strong and shall always flourish.

The 10 commandments for service providers to adults with autism

I have made the commitment to make a difference in the lives of others. This commitment is as much a part of me as my heart, eyes, and soul. While I will always seek to make a difference, I acknowledge the following:

1. *I will make mistakes.* The human spirit is complex. I cannot be prepared for every situation and unexpected behavior. But I will always learn from my experiences. I will be honest when I don't know what to do, and I will seek answers to the questions I cannot answer on my own. Most importantly, I will forgive myself for my errors and seek to avoid repeating them.

2. *I will change people's lives.* The work I do will not always yield immediate results. Sometimes months, even years will pass before I see the fruits of my labors. I still will not doubt my ability to make an impact on the lives of others, and I remain confident in my skills and abilities. Through my passion and patience, I will make the world a better place.

3. *I will always seek to see others fully for who they are.* In this line of work it is easy to focus on the disabling conditions and deficits. Sometimes they can seem insurmountable. But as I seek to look at each person fully, and to see what each individual can offer the world, I will also not seek outcomes that I know to be unrealistic. To falsely endorse a person's dreams when those dreams are impossible is disingenuous and cruel.

4. *I will always seek input from the person who has the disability.* I will not allow parents, guardians, or anyone else to steamroll over the people I work with; I will not allow others to silence their voices. I will not discuss their futures without them present, and I will not withhold

information from them to appease others. I will always seek and include their input, for their individual voices are the most important among them all.

5. *I will listen.* No matter how busy I am, no matter how many phone calls, emails, or tasks I face, the person I am working with will receive my undivided attention when we are together. I will tune out distractions, including those in my personal life, to ensure I hear what that person is telling me.

6. *I will seek to grow by learning from others.* Regardless of my education and training to date, I will always remember that this is an occupation that demands I continue to pay attention and learn every day. I must seek out new information. I will advocate with my employer for the opportunity to seek out professional development and periodically take sufficient time to update myself on new data and best practices. When I feel guilty taking time away from the people I serve, I will remind myself that increasing my knowledge will better empower me—and them—for the future.

7. *I will take care of myself.* The risk of burnout is high in my profession. The needs can be so great it can be difficult to take time off for myself and my family. I acknowledge that spending all my time on my work will one day lead to my undoing. I must be there for myself and not feel guilt when I have legitimate needs. With all the compassion I seek to express through my work, I must have that same compassion and patience with myself.

8. *I will appreciate the uniqueness of each person.* Every person is unique. Disabilities enhance individuality. So do age, race, gender, sexuality, ethnicity, personality, and life experiences. I will never generalize from one person to the next, and I will honor the beauty of the human experience by treating each person as a unique individual.

9. *I will seek input from others.* I realize that I will need others to help me empower others. Just as the child who is raised by the village becomes the most independent of all, so will the people I work with. I will always seek opportunities to encourage the growth of the circle of support that surrounds them—each additional voice seeking to empower them—so the person will become that much more independent and autonomous.

10. *I will never forget my passion.* There will be days when I will be very tired. I will hear a tragic story, encounter a near-hopeless situation, and feel a level of fatigue so great that all I will want to do is go home and sleep. On those days I will remember the passion that once called me to this field, and use it to once again make me strong.

Chapter 17

Concluding Thoughts

We're at the end of the book. Wow. If you stayed with me all the way through these pages, I cannot thank you enough. I'm not sure if my words have been helpful, but I sure hope so.

A final question comes to mind—what do I think the future will bring for education in general?

There will be some definite trends. For one, we will continue to see the number of spectrum students self-reporting in college rise. This is not to say that I believe the numbers are truly going up. In terms of diagnosis numbers, I think we have finally reached a satiation plateau, although in terms of statistics, there has been a steady growth in diagnoses of autism over the past 25 years. We know back in the 1980s that 1 out of 500 students was diagnosed with a spectrum disorder; in 2007 this became 1 out of 150, and most recently, 1 in 68 children (1 in 42 boys, 1 in 189 girls) have been diagnosed.[1] We also know that students on the autism spectrum currently make up approximately 15 percent of all college students with disabilities.[2]

So why are colleges seeing more students with disabilities than ever coming forward? For one, we have gotten better at diagnosing. Schools are better at seeing the signs, and parents, too, have greater recognition and understanding of the spectrum as it becomes more and more part of our cultural zeitgeist. I also believe that there is an over-identification effect in place. Having been in this field a long time,

---

1   CDC (Centers for Disease Control and Prevention) (2014) 'Autism Spectrum Disorder (ASD).' Accessed on 7/18/2017 at www.cdc.gov/ncbddd/autism/data.html

2   Horn, L. and Neville, S. (2006) *Profile of Undergraduates in Postsecondary Institutions: 2003–2004, with a Special Analysis of Community College Students.* Accessed 8/25/2017 at https://nces.ed.gov/pubsearch/pubsinfo.asp?pubid=2006184

disability diagnoses, like so many other things in society, can be trendy. For example, in the 1990s every other student I saw was diagnosed with some level of attention deficit disorder (ADHD). ADHD was the "diagnosis of the year," it seemed to me. Any student who had difficulty focusing or succeeding in school was suddenly an ADHD student.

I don't mean to say that many were not correctly diagnosed, but as human beings, when we encounter a behavior we don't understand, we like to label it. To us, as counselors and educators, the fact that a student isn't fully invested in his or her education seems wrong—we educated the student with all we have, so why would our students not give it their all? So we turn to the diagnosis. We see what we want to see because we need an explanation. I liken these misdiagnoses to horoscopes or the ancient dependence on Greek gods. When we lack an ability to explain something, we use whatever tools our imaginations allow to help us make sense of it.

Asperger's is the new ADHD in that it does help explain those students who perhaps struggle socially, have difficulty with organization, or aren't successful in high school without any other explanation. Sometimes there are disabling conditions at play that can also be confusing, such as anxiety or attention issues, and we mislabel the diagnosis as a result.

Another trend I am encouraged to see is more students taking pride in their diagnoses. Autism was something we poorly understood for so long, and we had very few overarching labels to explain it. In my generation, for example, when you heard autism, the primary response was to mention the movie *Rain Man*, in which Dustin Hoffman played an extremely high-functioning savant with an amazing ability to do things like count cards and he had an extraordinary memory for details, but socially his character could not carry out the most basic of conversations. Because of this depiction and others like it in popular culture, we associated autism with "different" and "unexplainable." Thus, socially, it was a thing that was pitied or frowned upon because the movie's lens encouraged us to wonder, "How can this person live a full life?" At the end of the movie, Dustin Hoffman's character is institutionalized, and so we assume this is how life ends for a person with his diagnosis—again, someone worthy of our pity.

But autism is entirely different for this generation. First, most young adults have never heard of the movie *Rain Man* or know its origins. Also, they are exposed to more young adults with the diagnosis and view it as just another trait that makes someone unique. I liken it to homosexuality. Research shows us the most common variable that determines someone's views on homosexuality is whether that individual knows a person who is gay. If we have a positive experience with a gay person, we view homosexuality positively.[3] The same can be said for the spectrum. Thus, students are more willing to self-identify and even seek out others like themselves not only online, but also in person.

This level of pride gives me great hope. While practitioners like me can offer insights, the unique observations of people themselves on the spectrum can, in many ways, be far more impactful and on target. I can write and speak all I want about how I *think* college and life can be for someone on the spectrum, but how can I ever fully know? Now, granted, you could say that even if you are on the spectrum the impact is still unique to each person, so even you will never have enough insight, but still, your view is closer to an understanding than I can ever achieve.

I think the final trend will be heightened levels of social exposure and stories of success, and social media plays a big role in this shift. We are seeing on reality shows characters openly on the spectrum talking about their experiences, and we are seeing more celebrities share their diagnosis—Tim Burton, Daryl Hannah, and Dan Ackroyd, to name a few. With this increased number of visible people with diagnoses, young adults are looking up to them and striving for success themselves.

Within education I think we will make a movement toward more multimodal instruction and thus meet the needs of more students than ever. We call this model "Universal Design"—direct, quantifiable suggestions that advance classrooms as universally fully accessible, designed by administrators and professors so that no student need

3   Morales, L. (2009) *Knowing Someone Gay/Lesbian Affects Views of Gay Issues*. Statistical Analysis Report, Gallup Poll Study, May. Accessed on 7/19/2017 at www.gallup.com/poll/118931/knowing-someone-gay-lesbian-affects-views-gay-issues.aspx

disclose a disability or accommodation needs in the first place. It is a relatively new model in education, with most literature on it less than ten years old. Universal Design theory is a good complement to the more nebulous Social or Minority Group Model in that it gives specific suggestions and actions that can be taken to make learning more accessible and create a positive learning climate. For example, Joan McGuire, Sally Scott, and Stan Shaw,[4] who wrote the nine principles of Universal Design, include concepts such as flexibility in use, simple and intuitive use, tolerance for error, and low physical effort, among others.

In essence, the idea of Universal Design is that if instruction is multimodal and planned from the very beginning, it is automatically accessible to *all* students regardless of whether they have a disability. For my doctoral dissertation I interviewed faculty who were labeled by students with disabilities as being the most effective. I found a lot of trends and ideas, but when I boiled it all down, they were all basically teaching in a Universally Designed framework, whether they realized it or not. Through the creativity and approachability of these teachers, more students were able to succeed than ever. My faith in the transformative ability of higher education, especially in community colleges where I work, makes me believe we will see more of this type of instruction in the future.

In conclusion, let us all remember that the first diagnosis of autism was only made relatively recently, in 1943, by psychologist Leo Kanner, and Asperger's syndrome was not an officially classified diagnosis by the American Psychological Association until 1994. Thus, in terms of length of study, these diagnoses are still relatively new, and we are learning more and more about the spectrum each day. I am hopeful that as time moves on we will learn more, and become more interconnected with one another through this sharing of understanding. This educational renaissance is happening now, and I am grateful to be a part of it. Thank you for reading.

---

4   McGuire, J., Scott, S. and Shaw, S. (2003) 'Universal Design for instruction: The paradigm, its principles, and products for enhancing instructional access.' *Journal of Postsecondary Education and Disability 17*, 1, 11–21.

Epilogue

Dr. Michael Duggan's Tips for Success in Higher Education and Life

1. *Always appreciate*—Whenever a person helps you, show you appreciate their help. When someone goes out of their way for a student, send a candy bar via campus mail or write a note. When they really, really go out of their way, send an email thanking them and copy their supervisor. People work hard and are often under-recognized. Give them the credit they deserve.

2. *Look for gaps in services*—Your unique vantage point helps you see what services students need that are missing. No student services division is ever complete. Find what's missing to help students, and then build mechanisms to support your programs. Never be complacent with statements like "that's just the way it is" or "we tried that once before and it didn't work."

3. *Seek out opportunities to work out of your department*—The best way to understand the college holistically and to build bridges is by working with people from other parts of the institution. Regularly seek out committees and other opportunities.

4. *Be the listener, not the talker*—Higher education is FILLED with people who have an opinion. The problem is that when you talk ALL the time at meetings, your words start to lose their value. Also, when you talk too much you tend to invest more time thinking about what to say next and can miss

others' ideas. Be the person who calmly listens and chimes in when you have something to say that really has meaning. It will add to the impact of what you say and increase credibility to your words.

5. *Never take interruptions when with students unless absolutely necessary*—Sometimes your phone and computer will ring off the hook and your instinct might be to interrupt the flow of conversation with your student to address it. Try not to do this. The most important person is the person in front of you. The call will wait. So will the email.

6. *Never let important ideas be forgotten*—Remember that higher education is slow. Very, very slow. Think how long it took from the day you applied to the day you were offered the job. Be patient. It's not a race. When you have good ideas and their implementation is slow, try to be patient but never let them die. Find ways to continue to bring them to the surface.

7. *Students need personal, genuine connections*—Having done this for 20+ years now, there are always articles about how "the generation X, Y, Z, Q learns." Read them, but don't take them too seriously. What really matters most is a human connection. Students will always seek people they can trust and who will listen. Be that person. Ask questions. When you see them again, show them you remembered your last conversation. Send occasional emails to all your students checking in. The minute a student decides they can trust somebody at the institution, their chances of success double. And don't be surprised if they keep in touch with you after graduation and beyond. I've written recommendation letters for law school, medical school, political offices, and even once a CEO for a tech company. Students remember connections, not grades.

8. *Seek out any and every opportunity to speak in front of others*— Higher education is a teaching profession. Speaking in front of others can be scary, especially at first. The bottom line, though,

is the better a public speaker you become, the more credibility you gather. Submit conference proposals, do workshops, teach classes, do anything to improve this skill.

9. *The people on the front lines are usually the hardest working and least appreciated ones out there*—The front desk areas of places like financial aid, counseling, cashiers, and registration can be like war zones. Students can lose patience and be disrespectful, parents can behave immaturely, and in many cases employees aren't given all the tools and authorizations to address the problems that come their way. Always, always show them appreciation. Learn their names. Thank them. Remember that without them, your job would a disorganized mess.

10. *Students are the best judge if you're doing a good job*—This is one of the best pieces of advice I ever got from an administrator. I was young and new on the job, just a couple of years, and I asked my dean, "Am I doing a good job?!?" Being the hard and enthused worker I was, I was confident she would say something nice. Instead, she said, "I don't know, ask your students." This couldn't be truer. There will be times YOU will be under-recognized, or misperceived, or forgotten by administrators and colleagues. When this happens, ignore it. You're not here for their approval. You're here for your students. Ask yourself if you're making a difference in their lives. If the answer is yes, then you're doing an excellent job, no matter what people on the periphery say or think.

11. *Don't be afraid to bend the rules or buck the system, a little*—Rules are meant to be broken when in the truest benefit of the student. Higher education is an incredibly complex system and there will always be exceptions. When there are, look for loopholes, if you must. Remember that adage of "it's always better to ask for forgiveness than for permission." *Sometimes* this will blow up in your face, but cumulatively over your career you will find you will score more victories for students than messes for you to clean up later.

12. *Assume the best about people, not the worst*—Yes, I understand the risks in doing this. Yes, at times students may lie to you and get away with it. Yes, co-workers might try to take advantage of you. But living a career with the philosophy of assuming "the world is out to get you" will turn you into a bitter, disconnected person. We all know those colleagues who fit the bill—and probably avoid them.

13. *Family and loved ones first*—Sometimes you will face tough decisions where you have to choose between work and family. Choose what matters the most. But when you make that choice, make it because you are *needed* by those you love, not just because you want to be needed. This is a critical differentiation. Calling in when your loved one is sick to take care of them is understandable. Asking to leave early, and thus requiring someone else to work late in your place so you can be home in time to make everyone dinner is not (you're too tired to cook anyways). Know the difference. Prioritize.

14. *Genuineness is key*—Say what you will about this generation, but one thing they can do from a mile away is tell when someone is insincere. The abundance of false truths and "alternate facts" is so heavy a student is very hesitant to trust anything an adult over 21 says. Be honest, even if it isn't what the student or parent wants to hear. And when you don't know something, admit it. Your honesty will be far more impactful than your lack of information.

15. *Don't take anything too seriously, and calm the hell down!*—I can't emphasize this enough. Of course, when your students' needs are on the line, do everything you can, but don't over-analyze comments from colleagues or look for hidden meanings to things. Don't be a victim. Don't get in a huff. Do your job. Help people. Leave work at work and enjoy your family. Save the drama for television.

16. *If you don't love it, quit. Please!*—Higher education is a competitive place. It's also an important place. Even if the financial loss for quitting is painful at first, it is worth it for your own longevity to look for something else that makes you happy. Bitterness can literally take years off your life. You owe it to both yourself and your students to look for something else if you don't like what you're doing. And don't think you can play it off—it's pretty easy to see who is passionate about their work and who is in it just for the paycheck.

Website and Resource Index

Chapter 1

www2.ed.gov/about/offices/list/ocr/504faq.html: United States Department of Education website summarizing the majority of legal protections afforded to adults with disabilities in higher education.

Chapter 2

www.ratemyprofessors.com: A website where students themselves rate instructors and include comments regarding their experiences with individual teachers. The site is not monitored (other than for racist/sexist/homophobic/abusive messages), and does not allow the faculty member to respond.

Chapter 4

www.michaelwduggan.com: My own personal website includes upcoming speaking engagements, current research of interest, and a message board where professionals and educators can post questions and share their wisdom and resources.

Chapter 7

www.bls.gov: The United States Department Bureau of Labor Statistics. Filled with accurate employment data and labor projections.

Chapter 8

www.cdc.gov/ncbddd/autism/facts.html: The Centers for Disease Control official current facts on autism.

Chapter 10

facebook.com/Autismerica and www.cod.edu/autismerica: The official Facebook (student-maintained) and College of DuPage (college-maintained) homepages of Autismerica.

Chapter 11

www.crccertification.com: The official website for the Commission on Rehabilitation Counselor Certification (CRCC).

Chapter 17

www.cdc.gov/ncbddd/autism/data.html: The Centers for Disease Control official current statistics on autism.

www.gallup.com/poll/118931/knowing-someone-gay-lesbian-affects-views-gay-issues.aspxC: The United States Gallup organization. Provides data and analytics on people in the US.

Contact Information

Thank you for taking the time to read my book. For contact information, or to visit my website, which includes a message board for posting and asking questions, please visit:

www.michaelwduggan.com

Or email:

michaelwduggan@yahoo.com

Index